D1277346

Trusting *Jesus* Every Day

Devotions to Increase a Woman's Faith

© 2016 by Barbour Publishing, Inc.

Print ISBN 978-1-63058-850-2

All rights reserved. No part of this publication may be reproduced or transmitted for commercial purposes, except for brief quotations in printed reviews, without written permission of the publisher.

Churches and other noncommercial interests may reproduce portions of this book without the express written permission of Barbour Publishing, provided that the text does not exceed 500 words or 5 percent of the entire book, whichever is less, and that the text is not material quoted from another publisher. When reproducing text from this book, include the following credit line: "From *Trusting Jesus Every Day*, published by Barbour Publishing, Inc. Used by permission."

Text previously published in *Secrets of Beauty, Secrets of Confidence, Secrets of Happiness,* and *Secrets of Serenity,* all published by Barbour Publishing, Inc.

Scripture quotations marked NIV are taken from the HOLY BIBLE, NEW INTERNATIONAL VERSION®. NIV®. Copyright © 1973, 1978, 1984, 2011 by Biblica, Inc.™ Used by permission. All rights reserved worldwide.

Scripture quotations marked KJV are taken from the King James Version of the Bible.

Scripture quotations marked NKJV are taken from the New King James Version®. Copyright © 1982 by Thomas Nelson, Inc. Used by permission. All rights reserved.

Scripture quotations marked NLT are taken from the Holy Bible. New Living Translation copyright© 1996, 2004, 2007 by Tyndale House Foundation. Used by permission of Tyndale House Publishers, Inc. Carol Stream, Illinois 60188. All rights reserved.

Scripture quotations marked CEV are from the Contemporary English Version, Copyright © 1995 by American Bible Society. Used by permission.

Scripture quotations marked MSG are from THE MESSAGE. Copyright © by Eugene H. Peterson 1993, 1994, 1995, 1996, 2000, 2001, 2002. Used by permission of NavPress Publishing Group.

Published by Barbour Books, an imprint of Barbour Publishing, Inc., P.O. Box 719, Uhrichsville, Ohio 44683, www.barbourbooks.com

Our mission is to publish and distribute inspirational products offering exceptional value and biblical encouragement to the masses.

Member of the
Evangelical Christian
Publishers Association

Printed in China.

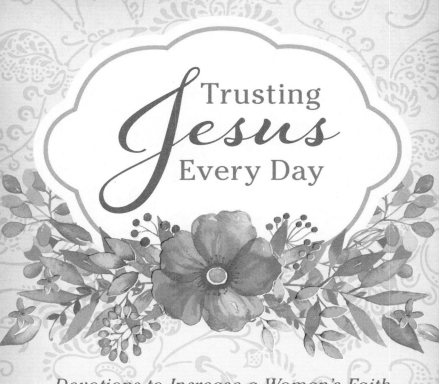

Trusting *Jesus* Every Day

Devotions to Increase a Woman's Faith

Michelle Medlock Adams
Katherine Douglas
Ramona Richards

BARBOUR BOOKS
An Imprint of Barbour Publishing, Inc.

Choose Trust

*Those who know your name trust in you,
for you, O LORD, do not abandon
those who search for you.*
PSALM 9:10 NLT

Trusting Jesus is easy on some days.

When you and the people you hold dearest are healthy. And gainfully employed. And generally happy. You've got–*er*–Jesus has got everything under control, right?

Except when things feel out of control. The car doesn't start. There's a rumor going around about downsizing at the company. A relationship crumbles. A bank forecloses. A routine test shows something suspicious.

But the fact is that Jesus is there in both scenarios. The Lord, the creator of the heavens and the earth, yearns for you to put your full, complete, total faith in Him. And that means choosing to trust Him *every day*.

What does that look like in your life? Think about some practical steps you can take to rely less on yourself (or a spouse, or a parent, or a friend) and rely more fully on God. Maybe that means stepping out of your comfort zone and sharing your faith with someone. Maybe it means following a dream that you've been too fearful to pursue.

Today, trust that Jesus has your back. Trust that He loves you, and He wants the absolute best for you today and always. He formed you to be the unique woman you are, and He wants you to live a life in Him– to the fullest!

God Turns Weaknesses into Strengths

· ·

Each time he said, "My grace is all you need.
My power works best in weakness." So now I am glad to boast about
my weaknesses, so that the power of Christ can work through me.
That's why I take pleasure in my weaknesses, and in the insults,
hardships, persecutions, and troubles that I suffer for Christ.
For when I am weak, then I am strong.
2 CORINTHIANS 12:9–10 NLT

*F*anny Crosby would no doubt agree with Paul's words about his
infirmities. Blinded when she was six weeks old by a man posing as a
doctor, she never wasted a moment in anger or self-pity, later writing,
"I have not for a moment in more than eighty-five years felt a spark
of resentment against him, because I have always believed that the
good Lord by this means consecrated me to the work that I am still
permitted to do."

A gifted, prolific poet, Fanny was already well-known for her
readings and published poetry by the time she was accepted at the
Institute for the Blind when she was fifteen. With a mind like
quicksilver, she memorized great works of literature, including most
of the Bible. She remained a student at the institute for twelve years,

then was a teacher there for eleven. All the while her poetry circled the globe, and the young girl found that by eighteen she was receiving visits from presidents and dignitaries.

At twenty-three she stood before the U.S. Congress, and at twenty-four published her first book. But she was not yet a Christian. Fanny had loved the language of the Bible, but its message had never opened her heart. Finally, at thirty-one, she received the Lord in a revival meeting, describing her own conversion as a flash of "celestial light." God touched her mind and soul, and the floodgates opened.

Over the next sixty years, Fanny wrote more than 8,500 hymns, sometimes as many as seven a day! Inspiration came to her from everywhere, from ordinary sources, such as a carriage ride, to events that rocked her life, like the death of her infant daughter, for whom she wrote "Safe in the Arms of Jesus."

What Fanny could not see, she could feel, and God's love and blessings on her set aside her blindness in favor of a wisdom and a "sight" that few other people have experienced. Yet all of us can follow her example in finding the confidence to use what gifts God has bestowed on us, no matter what "infirmities" challenge our everyday lives.

• •

A merry heart does good, like medicine.
PROVERBS 17:22 NKJV

Ever notice that when you smile it's like an instant face-lift? Your eyes look brighter. Your cheeks appear lifted. You just look better with a grin on your face. Not only does smiling make you look better, but also it is good for you–especially when your smile is accompanied by a chuckle or two.

According to information on the Discover Health website, by the time a child reaches nursery school, he or she will laugh about three hundred times a day. Know how many times a day an average adult laughs?

Only *seventeen* giggles a day, and that's just not enough. We need to laugh on a regular basis, and laughter starts with a smile.

Proverbs 17:22 says, "A merry heart does good, like medicine." In other words, laughter is good for your body. Laughter actually stimulates circulation, produces a sense of well-being, exercises the face and stomach muscles, stimulates the production of endorphins (the body's natural painkillers), and provides oxygen to the brain, to name a few benefits. Here are a few more facts to encourage your laughter:

- A few ha-ha's are good for your heart! According to a study at the University of Maryland Medical Center, laughter may actually help prevent heart disease. The study found that people with heart disease were 40 percent less likely to laugh in a variety of situations compared to people of the same age without heart disease.

- Giggling is a good workout! It has been proven that hearty laughter actually burns calories—as many as equivalent to several minutes on a rowing machine or an exercise bike. Now which would you rather do? Work out on a rowing machine or laugh awhile?

- Laughter can reduce stress! Laughter eases muscle tension and psychological stress, which keeps the brain alert.

- Last but not least, laughter makes you more attractive. People are naturally drawn to jolly people. Simply by wearing a smile, you become more approachable and better liked.

So go ahead. Smile. Chuckle. Giggle. Give a big ol' belly laugh, as they say in Texas. It's an instant makeover.

Refuge

· ·

*"May you be richly rewarded by the LORD, the God of Israel,
under whose wings you have come to take refuge."*
RUTH 2:12 NIV

*I*n the days when the judges ruled, there was a famine in the land"
(Ruth 1:1 NIV). That's how the book bearing Ruth's name begins.
It follows immediately on the heels of a book that ends with similarly
bleak words. "In those days Israel had no king; everyone did as they
saw fit" (Judges 21:25 NIV). From this setting a Jewish man and his
wife, Naomi, move to Moab. Ultimately their two sons marry women
of this country. And so begins the story of Ruth, the great-grandmother
of Israel's greatest king, David.

When Ruth, like her mother-in-law and sister-in-law, is widowed,
she decides to go to Israel with Naomi, her Jewish mother-in-law.
There's nothing to suggest that Ruth had ever visited or lived in Israel,
but she chooses to remain by Naomi's side and return there with
her. Something in the very first chapter of the book hints at Ruth's
source of serenity in a time often unkind to women–and in a culture
unfriendly toward Moabites, which is what Ruth was.

"Where you go I will go," she tells her mother-in-law. "Your people will be my people and your God my God. Where you die I will die, and there I will be buried. May the LORD deal with me. . .if even death separates you and me" (Ruth 1:16–17 NIV). Ruth's sureness of this move to unfamiliar country is not anchored in Naomi, but in the God she has come to call by His holy name–the Lord. She chooses to leave the familiar but pagan nature gods of her homeland to live with those who, like her, worship the one true God, the Lord God of Israel.

The love story between Ruth and an older man named Boaz dominates the rest of Ruth's story. Although Naomi encourages Ruth to work in the fields of Boaz for her own safety, Boaz himself tells Ruth that the God of Israel is the one under whose wings she has come to take refuge (Ruth 2:12). Ruth's future husband recognized that this young woman's serenity was not linked to his protection. It was linked to the Lord their God.

If we're facing a move to another city or country, our source of serenity can be the same as Ruth's. Not allowing the familiarity of the past or the uncertainty of the future to dictate our inner state allows God to work his peace in us. He "will keep in perfect peace all who trust in [him]" (Isaiah 26:3 NLT).

Drink Up!

*"Whoever believes in me, as the Scripture has said,
streams of living water will flow from within them."*
JOHN 7:38 NIV

Aqua. H_2O. Water. You can call it whatever you want as long as you drink lots of it. Water is one of the best beauty secrets in the world. Did you know that water suppresses the appetite naturally and helps the body metabolize stored fat? In other words, water helps you lose weight. So drink up!

Weight loss is just one of the benefits of drinking water. There are more reasons to drink H_2O: water carries needed nutrients through the body and carries unwanted waste out of the body. In other words, water helps cleanse your body internally. Need more convincing?

Here are some additional water facts to get you motivated:

- Water maintains blood volume and proper muscle tone.

- Water can improve the appearance of your skin.

- Water is a great treatment for fluid retention.

- Water keeps you from being dehydrated. (Did you know that

one of the most common reasons for headaches and anxiety attacks is dehydration?)

Ultimately, you should drink six to eight glasses of water every day. That's a good gauge, but here's an even better one. Try dividing your weight in half and drink that many ounces of water a day. That should be your goal.

Okay, now that you're convinced you should be drinking H_2O, I want to talk about another kind of water—the Living Water. If you've asked Jesus to be the Lord of your life, you're filled with the Holy Spirit, which is the Living Water. This water will make you beautiful on the inside and spiritually fit.

The Word talks of the Living Water in John 4. Remember the Samaritan woman Jesus met at the well? Because Jesus was a Jew and Jews didn't speak to Samaritans, she was shocked when He asked her for a drink of water. He said to her, "Everyone who drinks this water will be thirsty again, but whoever drinks the water I give them will never thirst. Indeed, the water I give them will become in them a spring of water welling up to eternal life" (vs. 13–14 NIV).

Let that Living Water stir on the inside of you today, and let it spill out onto all you encounter. You never know when "a Samaritan woman" might be watching and wondering what makes you different. When she asks "for a drink," you'll be able to offer her the Living Water that you've been given. That's one beauty secret you'll want to share!

Stand by Your Man

· ·

*Don't depend on things like fancy hairdos or gold jewelry
or expensive clothes to make you look beautiful. Be beautiful in your
heart by being gentle and quiet. This kind of beauty will last,
and God considers it very special.*

1 PETER 3:3–4 CEV

$\mathcal{R}$emember that old country song "Stand by Your Man"? (You're singing along right now, aren't you?) There's a lot of truth in that little melody. Whether you're engaged, married, or someday would like to have a special man in your life, this nugget of truth is for you. If you'll stand by your man and let him know that you are in his corner, adoring him, he will think you're the most beautiful woman in the world. Trust me!

Statistician and author Shaunti Feldhahn polled one thousand men about various topics for her book *For Women Only: What You Need to Know about the Inner Lives of Men*, so that we could better understand the men God has given us to love. When polled concerning their favorite movie scene of all time, the men overwhelmingly chose a scene from a baseball movie. You might be thinking that most men would've chosen a shoot-'em-up clip from some war movie. Not so. The most popular scene—the scene that evoked the greatest emotion from these one thousand men—came from *The Natural*. Remember that one, starring Robert Redford?

The scene goes something like this: Robert Redford is pitching, and the crowd is booing him and berating him. Redford steps off the mound and looks into the hostile crowd until his eyes lock on his woman, his gal, his love. She is quietly standing in support of him, smiling out of her eyes. In the midst of the chaos and screaming, he finds peace and strength and confidence simply by knowing she is in his corner, loving him and being proud of him.

That's what our men want. They want to know that we love them and support them—no matter what. They want to know that we still think they've got it going on. You say, "But I do think that. My husband knows I love him." Maybe he does, but maybe he needs to hear it more often. Or maybe he just needs to hear less criticism from you.

See, if we'll honor and adore our husbands, they'll love us like we need to be loved. It doesn't matter if our stomachs are a little pudgy or our teeth are a bit crooked; they'll see only the beauty in us. Start showing support and adoration to your man, and soon you'll become absolutely irresistible.

Friends Bring Happiness

* *

A friend loves at all times
PROVERBS 17:17 NIV

*F*riends. Television shows, hit songs, and countless stories have focused on the special people we call friends. Special occasions such as Friendship Week and Best Friend Day have even been established to honor them. Why? Because friends are important.

Friends are there for us in good times and bad. They support us when we need a shoulder to cry on. They encourage us when we need a boost of confidence. They celebrate with us when we accomplish our goals. They offer words of wisdom when we need advice. And, maybe most important, friends make life's journey a whole lot happier.

I can't imagine life without important gal pals. They are the thread of joy that runs through my life. From conversations about who is the best singer on *The Voice* to yummy pancake breakfasts at Cracker Barrel to all-day shopping trips to aerobic workouts on Saturday mornings–the times I spend with my best buddies bring me much joy.

Do you have special friends in your life? If so, how long has it been since you have taken time to get together with them, phone them, or drop them a card to say hello? Friendships take work. They require a time investment on your part. But they are definitely worth the time and effort. If you don't have any close friends with whom you can share your life, ask God to send you some of those precious people. Or if you have been neglecting your friends, determine today to rekindle those relationships.

God didn't intend for us to go through life alone. He knew we would need each other. He knew that friends would add a dimension of happiness to our lives that we wouldn't be able to get anywhere else. So celebrate your friends today—and enjoy the journey of life a little bit more.

Give God Control

. . . .

*For I know the thoughts that I think toward you,
says the LORD, thoughts of peace and not of evil,
to give you a future and a hope.*
JEREMIAH 29:11 NKJV

❦

𝒲e were moving to Indiana, from our Texas home, and we needed
a Realtor who could really work for us. We needed a Realtor who
would listen to our wants and dislikes and wholeheartedly search for
the perfect home for our family. We needed Pat.

I knew we were in good hands when I called her office and her
voice mail kicked on and said, "If you want to sell your home or
buy a new one, don't make a move without me. . . ." I liked that! I
thought, *Okay, I won't. I'm putting our home-buying experience in your
hands, Pat. You are in control.* Somehow that gave me such a feeling
of peace, just knowing that someone was working really hard on my
behalf. Suddenly, all of the pressure was off of my shoulders. It didn't
matter that I didn't know what properties were currently for sale or
which homes were going to become available in the near future, because
Pat was in the know. It's no wonder she has received numerous awards
in the realty world. She is good at what she does, and because of her

expertise, I could relax and let her do all the work. Whew! What a relief.

Well, guess what? I know someone who will work on your behalf—His name is Jesus, and if He had voice mail, His message would say: "Don't make a move without Me. . . ." You know what's so great about Him? He already knows your heart's desire, because He put those desires in you. And He wants to help you accomplish your dreams. He is constantly working behind the scenes for you. Isn't that a relief? See, we don't have to know everything as long as we know Him.

If you've been in the driver's seat too long, move over and let Jesus get behind the wheel. Let Him take total control of your life. If you do, you'll experience peace and satisfaction. You'll feel true joy just knowing that the Lord is on your side, desiring the very best for you. He'll lead you into good decisions. He'll guide you away from troubled times. He may even help you find your dream home! Your job? Let go and let God. In other words, don't make a move without the Lord. He has a beautiful life planned for you!

Who's Too Old?

*"I kept thinking, 'Experience will tell.
The longer you live, the wiser you become.' "*
JOB 32:7 MSG

*B*ible teacher Darlene Bishop said in one of her teachings, "God called me to teach the Word when I was only fourteen years old. I knew it. I heard that still small voice. But I didn't preach my first sermon until I was thirty-eight years old." She went on to say that in her early sixties, and she's more effective for God than she's ever been before. She's teaching more places, writing more books, and touching more lives than she ever thought possible. Bottom line–you're not too old to do what God has called you to do.

Today's society would have you believe that women past thirty should be put out to pasture. But that's simply not the case. God isn't concerned about our age, our wrinkles, or any gray hairs that might be sprouting. He just needs a willing vessel with a faithful heart.

Take Sarah in the Bible, for example. Abraham's wife thought she was too old to bear Abraham an heir. By the world's standards, she was well past childbearing years. Physically, it was impossible for her to conceive a child. But God had given her and Abraham a promise–

that Abraham would be the father of many nations. God didn't need Sarah's youthful body to produce a child. God just needed her faith and her willingness to be used. Once those were in place, she birthed Isaac–the promised heir.

Maybe you look into the mirror and see a woman who is too old to do anything worthwhile. Maybe you've bought the lie that the devil has been whispering in your ear: "You're too old to accomplish anything for God. Life has already passed you by. No one cares what an old woman has to say." If that's you, stop listening to the devil. He's a liar. You are not too old to do what God has planned for you. Like Darlene, you may be entering into your greatest days. We may be too old by Hollywood's standards, but we're just right by God's standards.

If you want to feel better about your mature appearance, you can color over your gray hair. You can even use antiwrinkle cream to combat those lines on your face. But you don't have to do those things to please God. He doesn't need a line-free face to do His work– only a willing heart. You're the perfect age to do what God has called you to do. So go for it!

God Is at Work

. . . .

*I am trusting you, O LORD, saying,
"You are my God!" My future is in your hands.*
PSALM 31:14–15 NLT

*D*id you know that God is often working most when we sense it the least?

As I reflect on my life, I can see that has often been the case. Those times when things looked the worst, when it seemed as if God had gone on vacation, were the times when God was working behind the scenes on my behalf.

We discover that our timing is not always God's timing. Actually, our timing is almost never God's timing. We want instant gratification in our give-it-to-me-now society. We want to pray and have God answer us by noon. But God usually doesn't work like that.

Take it from Noah. He followed God's leading and built an ark–even though it had never rained before. He obeyed God's instructions perfectly. Pairs of all the animals began to fill the big boat, and finally, Noah and his family boarded the ark and waited for the rain.

You know the story. It rained forty days and forty nights, and Noah and his family were the only ones spared. The boat ride, however, was much longer than forty days. It went on for months and months! Think about that for a moment: Noah and his family are on an ark with a bunch of smelly animals for months on end, and there's no land in sight. Can't you just hear his wife saying, "Yeah, great plan, Noah. Where's the land? Did God tell you how long we'd have to float around with a bunch of stinking creatures?"

You can imagine Noah, every day looking out the ark's windows, only to see water on every side. Finally, Noah sends out a bird, hoping to get proof that land has appeared somewhere–but the bird comes back empty-beaked. It must have looked like God had forgotten them, that they were doomed to ride around on a big boat forever.

But God was at work, slowly diminishing the water every day– even those days when Noah saw water all around. In time the ark hit dry land, and Noah and his family left the ark to enjoy God's promise.

Are you on a long ark ride right now? If so, rejoice! Be happy today–even if you can't see anything changing. Land is near. God hasn't forgotten you. He is at work behind the scenes.

As a Little Child

. . . .

*The wolf will live with the lamb, the leopard will lie down with
the goat, the calf and the lion and the yearling together;
and a little child will lead them.*
ISAIAH 11:6 NIV

*T*oddler Gabrielle does have a favorite holiday, but it's not
Halloween. When scary goblins, ghosts, and monsters start making
their appearance at the end of October, usually gregarious Gabrielle
hides behind her mother's legs. That gives her a moment of perceived
safety, but that isn't where she finds her peace. Her mother overheard
this spontaneous burst of prayer as soon as they got into the car.
"Dear Jesus, You know I scared of those monsters. They are bad. I no
like them. Please keep me safe, Jesus. Don't let them hurt me. I know
You keep me safe, Jesus. I know You do." Without an amen, but
with the confident faith of a child, Gabrielle made the instantaneous
transition back to her usual talkative, happy self.

Think back to when you were a little girl. Did you worry about
getting to Grandma's when it was snowing? Hardly. The truth was
plain and simple: *we're going to Grandma's!* And, better than best,
it was snowing, too! Did you stew for hours over what to wear to a

party? No. You were thrilled to be invited! Did you worry about dog hair in the house? Hardly–you were tickled that you got to have a puppy all your own!

It didn't take much back then to keep us content. When Jesus wants us to consider contentment, He tells us to check out growing things–lilies and children, to name two. "And why do you worry about clothes? See how the flowers of the field grow. They do not labor or spin. Yet. . .not even Solomon in all his splendor was dressed like one of these" (Matthew 6:28–29 NIV).

When critical adults grew angry with rambunctious children in the temple area, Jesus reminded them that it's "from the lips of children and infants" that God ordains praise (Matthew 21:16 NIV). Particularly when the praise is spontaneous.

How do we do that? How do we get hold of the selfless contentment of children? How do we content ourselves when the commonalities of life bog us down in frustration and worry? Christ says to remember that God knows all about our daily needs. What we must do is "seek first his kingdom and his righteousness." Then "all these things will be given to [us] as well" (Matthew 6:33 NIV).

Set the Right Tone

· ·

Your godly lives will speak to them without any words.
They will be won over by observing your pure and reverent lives.
1 PETER 3:1–2 NLT

$\mathcal{R}$emember when you first started dating your significant other? You couldn't wait to see each other. You thought he was so handsome, and he thought you were absolutely gorgeous. It was butterflies and sunshine every time you were together, right? Then. . .something happened. Suddenly, the little quirky habits you thought were so cute about one another weren't so cute anymore. He began acting distant, and you began nagging. After a while he didn't seem quite so handsome, and now he rarely tells you that you're beautiful.

That's where many couples find themselves today, which is why many women feel so unattractive and depressed. Women's magazines tell us to spice up our marriages with new lingerie. So we run to Victoria's Secret and realize that only Victoria looks good in most of those outfits. Just how do we become attractive again to that person who used to adore us?

We have to set the right tone.

When I got married, I quickly discovered that I didn't love

26

everything about my spouse—at least not all of the time. It was one of those days when I settled into my chair at women's Bible study. I sulked as our teacher began her lesson on 1 Peter 3. *Oh, no,* I thought. *Not the "submission lesson." Not today!*

She began by saying, "Wives, *you* set the tone in the home." I never heard much past that statement because that one nugget of truth grabbed hold of my heart and wouldn't let go. I realized that I didn't have to look like Angelina Jolie to be attractive to my mate. It wasn't even about my appearance. It was about my attitude toward my mate. I decided that day to take Monda's words of wisdom and apply them to my home. Instead of nagging, I would find reasons to compliment my mate. Instead of just saying good-bye in the morning, I would give him a big kiss to start the day. Guess what? Things got better immediately.

No, I don't get it right every day, but after fourteen years of marriage, I'm a much better tone setter than I used to be! If your spouse is less than crazy about you as of late, or if you long to have your husband look at you the way he once did—through adoring eyes— you have to change your attitude. Meditate on 1 Peter 3 and begin setting the right tone today. Soon your home will be heavenly and your husband will refer to you as "his beautiful angel."

Learning to Listen

. . . .

"Be still, and know that I am God."
PSALM 46:10 NIV

*L*et's face it. We like to talk. The *Farmer's Almanac* reports that
the average woman speaks twenty-five thousand more words per day
than the average man. No wonder the men in our lives "tune us out"
from time to time. Listening is almost a lost art form today. The late
Brenda Ueland, a prolific Minnesota author and columnist, once
wrote: "We should all know this: that listening, not talking, is the
gifted and great role, and the imaginative role. And the true listener
is much more beloved and magnetic than the talker, and she is more
effective and learns more and does more good."

My friend Darlene recently learned how attractive good listening
skills can be. She sat next to a woman at her son's ball game, and
since she'd never met the woman before, Darlene asked her several
questions. The woman answered her inquiries all night long—never
once asking Darlene to share any information in return.

Later that week, the gabby woman's daughter told Darlene how
much her mother had enjoyed their conversation at the ball game.
Darlene had to smile at the daughter's comment. It had been a one-sided

conversation, but apparently it was just what the woman had needed, and Darlene was glad to have obliged.

Many times, we're so eager to share our witty comments or tell a funny story to make ourselves seem more attractive that we don't actually listen to the speaker. No, we're too busy "rehearsing" our responses in our minds, waiting for the first opportunity to interrupt and dazzle those around us.

Are you guilty of interrupting? Do you lack listening skills? If you're like most women, you do. And that's not a very attractive trait. No matter how pretty you might be on the outside, if you're constantly interrupting and talking over others, people will not see you in a good light.

People love a good listener–especially the men in our lives. If you'll hang on his every word, he'll talk to you more often. Practice listening today. You just might learn that talking is way overrated.

Edible Serenity

• •

*Taste and see that the L*ORD *is good.*
PSALM 34:8 NIV

$\mathcal{T}$ry as I might, I can't find a single reference to chocolate in the Bible. Not a hint of cocoa or that sorry second, carob. The closest thing to chocolate in the Bible is honey–golden, stick-to-your- fingers honey. Golden chocolate, you might say. When we want a taste of edible delight, most of us reach for chocolate. I've yet to meet a woman who finds sweet consolation in a celery stick or a carrot. And let's be honest: an apple or an orange is just a guiltless substitution for the real thing.

No, when we girls want a serenely satisfying treat, we reach for the Snickers–or at least a shoe-size block of baklava. Oh, such sweet, heavenly savor. . . Sweet serenity for the soul is not linked to our taste buds, but to God. The psalmist says God's words to us are "sweeter than honey, than honey from the honeycomb" (Psalm 49:40 NIV). But sometimes the sweet pleasure of God's teaching can disagree with us. In the book of Revelation, John says, "I took the little scroll from the angel's hand and ate it. It tasted as sweet as honey in my mouth, but when I had eaten it, my stomach turned sour" (Revelation 40:40

NIV). The whole counsel of God brings us both satisfying peace and hard-to-digest truth.

Jesus encouraged us to enjoy a soul feast of Him. "I am the bread of life. Whoever comes to me will never go hungry, and whoever believes in me will never be thirsty" (John 6:35 NIV). Not only is Jesus true soul food, but He is soul drink as well. "Whoever drinks the water I give them will never thirst. Indeed, the water I give them will become in them a spring of water welling up to eternal life" (John 4:14 NIV). Christ wraps up His shocking statements simply. "The one who feeds on me will live because of me. . . . Whoever feeds on this bread [meaning Himself] will live forever" (John 6:57–58 NIV).

Need a sweet fix today? Need a serenity fix? The Lord invites us to feast on Him and His words. "How sweet are your words to my taste," exclaimed the psalmist, "sweeter than honey to my mouth!" (Psalm 119:103 NIV). Find a spot and curl up with God's Word to start, end, or even get through the hump part of your day. Feast on the One who is the "true bread from heaven" (John 6:32 NIV)–and maybe grab a *small* handful of M&Ms while you're at it. Very small. Very, very, very small. Then chow down some spiritual and some physically edible serenity!

Worms and All

• •

*Not that I have already obtained all this, or have already
arrived at my goal, but I press on to take hold of that
for which Christ Jesus took hold of me.*
PHILIPPIANS 3:12 NIV

*D*o you ever feel overwhelmed, as if you are about to be buried in
the pile of mounting laundry in your hamper? Have you ever felt like
everyone at work thinks you're a moron in a nice outfit? Do you ever
feel like twenty-four hours is simply not enough time to accomplish
everything on your to-do list? There are times when I feel so overwhelmed
and ill-equipped that I just want to run and hide under the bed. Then I
think, *But God is God. He knew all of my shortcomings and faults before
He entrusted me with all of these responsibilities, so He must see potential
in me that I don't.*

Aren't you thankful that God looks at us through eyes of love
instead of condemnation? On the days when I lose my temper with
my family or fail to meet a work deadline or miss an opportunity to
witness for Him simply because I'm too exhausted from the day-to-
day burdens, I am immensely thankful that God is a patient, loving,
always-seeing-the-best-in-me kind of God. I am not a perfect mother.

I mess up at work sometimes. And I often bite off more than I can chew. But God is changing me and perfecting me from glory to glory. And He is doing the same for you!

He understands when we miss the mark. He cheers us on when we take a step closer to Him. He actually loves us even when we are at our very worst. Think about that for a moment. God loves us so much that He gave His only Son for us—in spite of our shortcomings and less-than-perfect moments.

So the next time you feel overwhelmed, less than worthy, and totally clueless, ask God to help you see yourself the way He sees you. He adores you. You're the apple of His eye—even if you are a bit wormy at times. Now that's something to be happy about!

Blind Faith

I am sure that nothing can separate us from God's love—
not life or death, not angels or spirits,
not the present or the future.
ROMANS 8:38 CEV

Let's be honest. There are some beauty tricks that simply don't make sense if you think about them too long. In fact, some of them are downright gross. For instance, if you have tired, puffy eyes from too many sleepless nights, you're supposed to pat a little Preparation H under your eyes to reduce the puffiness and rejuvenate your tired peepers. Yes, it's quite effective, but did you ever think you'd use hemorrhoid cream around your eyes? Me either! Or how about the old Vaseline-on-the-teeth trick? Beauty queens have known about this tip for years! You simply put a little slimy Vaseline over your front teeth to create a shinier smile onstage. Of course it feels yucky, but it works!

Sometimes you just have to have blind faith and try these odd beauty tricks. There's no rhyme or reason to them, and they may even seem gross to you. But if you try them, you'll discover they actually work.

You know, some of the teachings in the Bible seem odd, too.

Take Matthew 5:38–41, 44 (NIV), for example. Instead of an "eye for eye, and tooth for tooth," we are supposed to love our enemies: "You have heard that it was said, 'Eye for eye, and tooth for tooth.' But I tell you, do not resist an evil person. If anyone slaps you on the right cheek, turn to them the other cheek also. And if anyone wants to sue you and take your shirt, hand over your coat as well. If anyone forces you to go one mile, go with them two miles. . . . Love your enemies and pray for those who persecute you."

Hmm. Not exactly what human nature tells us to do, right? Sometimes you just have to trust and go forward in blind faith. If you're a very practical person, this might be hard for you, so ask God to help you follow His ways even when they seem outlandish or uncomfortable. He will! He is the Father of faith, and He has more than enough to fill you up so that you can step out in blind faith and love your enemies, pray for those who despitefully use you, and go that extra mile.

So take a risk. Go against your human nature and step out in blind faith both in the natural and the spiritual. You'll have rested eyes, shiny teeth, and a beautiful spirit!

A Winning Look

*No, in all these things we are more than
conquerors through him who loved us.*
ROMANS 8:37 NIV

*A*hh. . .the dreaded last word. Are you a gotta-have-the-last-word kind of gal? Do you always have to be right? If so, you're not alone. I am also a member of that club, and let me tell you, it's a pretty lonely and sad membership. When you always have to be right, people tend to shy away from you. They will conveniently have an excuse "not to see you" every time you want to get together. And can we blame them? What our mothers used to tell us is really true–pretty is as pretty does. If you act ugly, people will view you as ugly, and they won't want to be around you.

So if we know that having to have the last word makes us unattractive, why do we continue in this behavior? Because we are taught that winning is everything. We're taught, "Nice guys (and gals) finish last." We're told, "If you don't look out for number one, who will?" But those teachings are directly opposed to the Word of God.

Don't get me wrong–Jesus is all about winning, but not at someone else's expense. The Bible says that He has made us more

36

than conquerors. (Sounds like God is in the business of making winners, doesn't it?) He wants us to succeed, but He wants us to do it His way. When we do it His way, we'll still have friends when we arrive at that all-important winner's circle.

So stop looking out for "number one" and start looking to *the* One! Let Him mold you into the beautiful creature He's created you to be! Determine to change your ugly ways. Realize that you don't have to get the last word in. His Word is word enough. And begin following in Jesus' footsteps. His steps always lead to victory, and you'll look good on the journey!

Bring on the Breakthroughs!

. . . .

And I am certain that God, who began the good work within you,
will continue his work until it is finally finished on
the day when Christ Jesus returns.
PHILIPPIANS 4:6 NLT

𝓜y mother-in-law has used Merle Norman cosmetics for many years. Trends in cosmetics come and go, but she sticks with her tried-and-true line. Sure, over the years she's tried products from other beauty companies, but she always returns to her favorite–Merle Norman.

Women are funny about those kinds of things. When we get used to something and it works for us, we are very resistant to change. Even if a beauty breakthrough occurs, even if a "new and improved" line is launched, and even if our best friend starts selling a different product line, we'd rather just stick with what we've been using for years. Like the old expression goes: "If it ain't broke, why fix it?"

While this line of thinking might be okay when it comes to our cosmetic choices, it can be quite dangerous in the spiritual realm. A few years ago I was attending a traditional denominational church and a battle in the vestibule broke out. We'd hired a new music minister, and he was full of energy and new ideas. Instead of only leading the congregation in hymns from our tattered old red hymnbooks, he began leading us in contemporary worship choruses. All of us thirty and younger loved the new contemporary worship, while most of the elder members—not so much. It became a clash of the choruses. The elderly population was adamantly against the worship music shift. One of the board members finally spoke up and said, "We've sung these hymns for years. If they were good enough for the founders of this church, they're good enough for me."

Eventually, the bright-eyed praise and worship leader was forced to lead the congregation in old hymns—period. It caused great division in our congregation, and several families left the church due to the immense tension.

As Christians we need to be open to new things—as long as those new things are of God. Ask God to give you discernment so that you can go with the flow as long as that flow is from the Father. Don't be resistant to change. Maybe God is trying to help you grow in an area but your resistance is slowing up the process. I say, bring on the beauty breakthroughs and latest skin-care technology, and bring on the new spiritual revelations and levels of maturity. We're on our way to becoming better—inside and out!

Flex Those Muscles!

. . . .

Train yourself to be godly. For physical training is of some value,
but godliness has value for all things, holding promise
for both the present life and the life to come.
1 TIMOTHY 4:7–8 NIV

$\mathcal{F}$or many of us a good workout brings a measure of balance to our lives. Whether it's aerobics, lifting, biking, or running, exercise is good for both our bodies and our heads. When we glide down a pristine slope in winter's snow or breathe deep of awakening spring during a toning walk, a sense of mental calm can overtake us even as our bodies glisten (men are the ones who *sweat*) and our hearts pump to keep the pace. We may not wear a satisfied smile on our faces while we firm it up and trim it down, but rumor has it we'll sleep better come bedtime.

For those of us who thrive on routine physical exercise, it's reassuring to know that God tells us our trek around the track isn't wasted time. "Of some value" in the Greek means exercise is useful, advantageous, profitable, and helpful. To study the letters of Paul the apostle is to meet a man who alludes to sports and physical exercise frequently. He compared himself spiritually to an athlete in training for the Greek games of his day–our modern-day Olympic games (see 1 Corinthians 9:24–27).

With all that said, the Bible takes us one step further. We may find focus and release in physical exercise. That's because physical exercise is good for us. "But godliness," we're also told, "has value for *all things*" (emphasis added). The kicker? We have to train ourselves to be godly. Excuse me? How in the world do we train ourselves in godliness? There's serenity in that?

We must "turn to God in repentance and have faith in our Lord Jesus" (Acts 20:21 NIV). We ask God's forgiveness for our sin and disobedience against Him. We trust in Christ who "died for our sins according to the Scriptures" and who "was raised on the third day according to the Scriptures" (1 Corinthians 15:3–4 NIV). As we then "continue to work out [our] salvation with fear and trembling. . .it is God who works in [us] to will and to act in order to fulfill his good purpose" (Philippians 2:12–13 NIV).

The final result brings a win-win situation for our spiritual and our physical well-being. "A heart at peace gives life to the body" (Proverbs 14:30 NIV)–that's better than a two-hour marathon!

A Beautiful Aroma

*In fact, God thinks of us as a perfume that brings Christ
to everyone. For people who are being saved, this perfume
has a sweet smell and leads them to a better life.*

2 CORINTHIANS 2:15–16 CEV

$\mathcal{S}$he breezed in and sat down in front of me at an Indiana University basketball game on that cold February night. She was an older woman, dressed in a navy business suit, with a red-and-white scarf tied stylishly around her neck. Her silver hair was neatly tucked behind her ears in a classic bob, and her lipstick was a perfect IU crimson color.

I would have guessed her to be in her early fifties–probably an IU professor. As she settled into her seat, a wonderful aroma filled the air. It broke through the smells of stale popcorn and overcooked hot dogs and filled my nostrils. I inhaled deeply and said, "Mmmm."

"Do you smell that?" I whispered to my mother.

"Yes, it's marvelous," she answered.

There was no doubt. The wonderful aroma had wafted in with the classy lady in front of us. As the halftime buzzer sounded, I leaned forward and tapped the woman on her shoulder.

42

"Excuse me, ma'am. You smell so wonderful. Could you tell me what you're wearing?"

"Thank you," she said, then told me the name of her perfume.

I shared the information with my mother, and we each made a mental note about our next perfume purchase. I wanted to smell just like the classy lady with the silver hair.

You know, the Bible says we are the aroma of Christ. When we enter a room, we should carry His fragrance with us. His aroma should be so pleasing on us that people will tap us on the shoulder and ask, "Excuse me, ma'am. You smell wonderful. What are you wearing?" With that opening, we can share Jesus Christ with every person who notices our Christlike aroma.

Maybe your fragrance smells more like those overcooked weenies or stale popcorn. If so, you just need a "smell makeover." Ask God to replace your human smell with His divine fragrance so that you will be a witness of His sweetness everywhere you go. Ask the Lord to fill you with His fragrant love so that it enters the room even before you do. He will. He doesn't want His children to go around smelling stinky. After all, we are the aroma of Christ, and that's better than the finest perfume.

The Confidence to Risk Everything

· ·

*So they went, and came to the house of a harlot named Rahab,
and lodged there. . . . Then the woman took
the two men and hid them.*

JOSHUA 2:1, 4 NKJV

*A*ny woman who thinks she needs to perfect her life or faith before
serving the Lord should take another look at Rahab. One of the
women named in the record of faithful heroes (see Hebrews 11:31),
Rahab's early life hardly appeared to be a model-perfect picture of
morality and belief.

Her growing faith in the works of the Lord, however, gave her the
confidence to put everything she knew at risk.

Rahab's life could not have been easy. The text refers to her as
a prostitute, although some archaeological evidence indicates Rahab
may have operated an inn, since the two jobs were often closely
linked and scripture says that the spies lodged with her. Either way,
her profession was difficult and dangerous. Yet Rahab met a lot of
travelers, and she had learned in great detail what was going on in her
city as well as her country. Thus, while Rahab's decision to hide the
Hebrew spies on her roof may seem a bit impulsive as first told in

Joshua 2, she later makes it clear that this is something she'd been thinking about for some time.

When ordered by the king to surrender the spies, she quickly hid the men on the roof and covered them with flax. She then explained to the king's messenger that the spies had already departed, risking a charge of treason. After the king's men left, however, Rahab confronted the two Israelites about what the Lord had been doing and asked for their help (see Joshua 2:8–13). She had been listening to her clients and marveling at all the Lord had done in Canaan. Although other citizens of Jericho probably knew as much as she did about the conquests of Israel, this quick-thinking and intelligent woman was the only one to put more faith in God than the fortifications of her city. Believing instead that Jericho would never stand against the power of God, Rahab chose to follow the Lord, no matter what the cost.

Her faith saved her family–and this strong woman became one of the ancestors of Jesus Christ. Her example reminds us today that no matter what our background or circumstances, what God wants most of all is simply our trust and love.

A Beautiful New You

• •

Anyone who belongs to Christ is a new person.
The past is forgotten, and everything is new.
2 CORINTHIANS 5:17 CEV

I recently saw an infomercial for a skin-care system called ProActiv that is guaranteed to help those who suffer from acne. During this infomercial, a skin-care specialist explained how blemishes start beneath the skin two weeks before they ever manifest on one's face. That's why, she said, we should treat acne before it shows itself on the surface. By treating the pimples before they ever show up on the surface of the skin, the skin is consistently clear. Problem skin becomes a thing of the past. Testimonial after testimonial confirmed that the products worked. Finally, I was convinced. I ordered the products for my "tweenage" daughters, hoping to help them avoid the perils of pimples that typically go along with adolescence.

You know, products like ProActiv may take care of the pimples that pop up on our faces and bodies, but the Word of God takes care of the blemishes of the heart. And you don't have to order it off of an infomercial. It's free, and it's for you! Hurt and bitterness are much like those hidden pimples that lie deep beneath the surface. They may lie dormant for weeks, but eventually they will pop out and cause all kinds of problems.

If you've been harboring hurt or buried bitterness in your heart, let God's Word go to the root of those issues and zap them. If you don't, hurt feelings will present themselves at the most inopportune times. Hurt will rear its ugly head—just when you think you've gotten rid of it forever. So read God's Word on a regular basis and keep your heart continually clear. If you don't, hurt and bitterness and all of its ugly buddies will erupt in your life again and again and again. Don't let that happen! Be proactive! Get in the Word of God and unveil a more beautiful version of you!

"Don't Hate Me Because I'm Beautiful"

. . . .

Yet you are stupid enough to brag,
and it is wrong to be so proud.
JAMES 4:16 CEV

You've seen the commercial. The gorgeous girl whips her long, luscious locks to the side, then with her pouty, very glossy lips, she utters, "Don't hate me because I'm beautiful."

But in reality, we would hate her–not because she's beautiful. No, we'd hate her because she loves to brag on herself. Let's face it; nobody likes a bragger. (You're thinking of someone right now, aren't you?) We all know someone like that girl in the commercial. She might not be as blatant, but you can bet your lipstick she'll find a way to sneak in a boast or two.

She might not even brag about herself. She might brag about her new home. Or worse, she might drone on and on about her super-accomplished kids. (Her car bumpers are covered with MY KID IS AN HONOR STUDENT stickers. Okay, I have those bumper stickers, too. Sorry.) No matter what she brags about, it's enough to make you want to run for the hills. Am I right?

Let me ask you another question. Are you a bragger? Do you love talking on and on about yourself? It's an easy habit to fall into, but it's also a very dangerous one. The Bible says that pride comes before a fall, and that fall may plop you right into a pit of loneliness. Friends will start avoiding you. Family members will dread your annual brag letter, er um, Christmas letter. People will hate you–but it won't be because you're beautiful. So don't go there!

If you're struggling with the bad habit of bragging, ask God to put a watch over your mouth. Make a conscious decision to listen more than you talk. And more than anything, learn to trust God to raise you up. You'll discover that you won't have to brag on yourself to feel important. God has a big ol' brag book, and He will find ways to lift you up and give you favor with those around you. You'll win friends and influence people, and they'll love you because you're beautiful on the inside. After all, that's where it really counts!

Singing the Blue Jeans Blues

· ·

*Not that I have already obtained all this, or have already
arrived at my goal, but I press on to take hold of that
for which Christ Jesus took hold of me.*

PHILIPPIANS 3:12 NIV

We've all been there. You go to the mall with high hopes and high self-esteem, ready to buy a new pair of jeans. Seventy-two pairs later, your legs are raw from trying them on and your self-esteem is lower than a snake's belly. Sadly, you leave the mall, determined to work out seven times a day and eat only lettuce until the next time you get the courage to try on jeans once again.

Jeans are a part of every gal's wardrobe, but finding a pair that fits every curve and hides every bulge can be quite challenging. Wouldn't it be great if jeans were labeled something like this: "If you have short legs, these jeans are for you," or "If your thighs are heavy, try these." Okay, so the marketing pitch might need a little work, but honest labels would enable women of every build to find the right jeans.

Still, we press on–determined to find the jeans that won't make our hind ends look flat and wide. Sometimes this quest may take days, even weeks. But, eventually, we will succeed. We're women–shopping challenges don't faze us.

If only we were that determined and steadfast when it comes to other areas of our lives—especially spiritual battles. If you're like me, you sometimes get weary in the well-doing. Have you found yourself throwing in the faith towel before you see your victory come to pass?

It's easy to do. Evangelist Chip Brim once shared that God had shown him a vision of Christians on a football field. They were all collapsing on the one-yard line. They were so close to their break-throughs, but they simply grew weary and quit just inches from their victory.

Chip said it made him very sad to see so many Christians giving up on their dreams or quitting before they'd realized their breakthroughs. I've got news for you. It makes God sad, too. He longs to see His children walk in abundance in every area of their lives. He has already paid the price for your victory! You just have to push toward that goal—no matter how hard it gets. The Bible says all things are possible for those who love the Lord. The Bible says you can do all things through Christ Jesus. Don't quit just short of your victory. The end zone is in sight! And the reward is even better than finding that perfect pair of blue jeans. So don't give up!

Blossom Where You're Planted

*For everything there is a season,
a time for every activity under heaven.*
ECCLESIASTES 3:1 NLT

I have a friend named Barbie who is an excellent writer. She currently works as a columnist and reporter for a daily newspaper. It's a high-stress job. The newsroom is a frantic, wonderful, wacky place to work. I know because I used to work at that same daily newspaper several years ago. Deadlines loom. Bosses demand. And the news never stops. The news doesn't care if your daughter has a dance recital. It still has to be written right away. Being a newspaper reporter is the worst job you'll ever love. Long hours. Disgruntled readers. Difficult sources. You'll deal with them all on a daily basis, but at the end of the day, you'll know you've contributed to a greater cause. You'll know you've made a difference. If just one person is touched by a story you wrote for page B-3, then it was all worth it.

Still, it's tough. There are days when my friend longs to escape the daily rat race and write Christian books and children's stories from her home office. But there is a season for everything, and Barbie is blooming right where she is planted. She isn't blatant about her faith, but you can just tell when you read her stories that there's a Christian pecking away at that computer. Her stories touch your heart, make you think, and challenge you to be a better person.

Let me ask you–are you blooming where you're planted? If your dream is to stay home with your children and yet you're stuck in a customer service job somewhere, are you blossoming on the job? Do you smile and earnestly try to help your customers, or do you grumble around, complaining that you'd rather be home with your babies? No matter what season of life you're in, you should bloom. Ask God to help you do the best you can. Ask Him to help you be a blessing wherever you are. Ask God to give you the patience and love to blossom–even if you're among a bunch of ungodly weeds. Just think, you might be the only Christian those weeds will ever see.

Joyce Meyer once said, "Enjoy the journey on the way to where you're going." That's good advice. You'll be a lot happier, and you'll be a lot more attractive to those who are around you. So go ahead– bloom!

Step into Your Dreams

· ·

God's Spirit doesn't make us slaves who are afraid of him.
Instead, we become his children and call him our Father.
ROMANS 8:15 CEV

*I*n the early 1950s, Lillian Vernon spent five hundred dollars on her first advertisement, offering monogrammed belts and handbags. That one little ad, that one little risk, produced a $32,000 profit! Today—more than fifty years later—Lillian Vernon is still selling gift items and personalized goodies through a very successful catalog sales program. In fact, her company now generates more than $250 million in sales every year. Now that's a lot of handbags!

She has quite a success story. But what if Lillian Vernon hadn't run that small ad? Back then, five hundred dollars was a lot of money to spend with no guarantee of recouping it. What if she hadn't taken that risk? Well, she wouldn't be a millionaire, and lots of folks would have to find another catalog to use for their annual Christmas shopping.

Maybe God has put a dream in your heart that is so big you haven't even shared it with anyone. Maybe God is directing you to take a risk in business or start your own Bible study or volunteer for your child's school or run for office. So what's stopping you? Why aren't you running that ad like Lillian Vernon? Why aren't you going for it?

If you're like most women, fear is holding you back. Fear is a very real emotion. It can get a grip on you that won't let go—until you make it let go through the Word of God. The Bible tells us that "God has not given us a spirit of fear" (2 Timothy 1:7 NLT). So if it didn't come from God, where did it come from? Satan, maybe? You bet. So get rid of that nasty old emotion.

Say out loud, "I can do all things through Christ who strengthens me. I am the head and not the tail. I am more than a conqueror." Remind yourself of who you are in Christ Jesus on a daily basis. You are a child of the Most High King. You have the mind of Christ. God has crowned you with His favor. And those are just a few of the promises in His Word. So grab hold of God's promises, put fear behind you, and step into your dreams. Pretty soon you'll be sharing your success story!

No Divas Allowed!

*"Here is a simple, rule-of-thumb guide for behavior:
Ask yourself what you want people to do for you,
then grab the initiative and do it for them."*
MATTHEW 7:12 MSG

𝒟o you love to read gossip magazines? You know, the ones on the racks right by the checkout lanes in the grocery store? I confess–I read them. And do you know what is in most every issue? A diva report. These tabloid journalists follow stars around and let us know which stars are nice and which ones are dastardly divas. You discover which stars care very little about "the little people" and which famous folks do very nice things for the people in their lives–even those who serve them.

I am a huge Doris Day fan. When I was pregnant with my daughter Abby, I was sentenced to bed rest for several weeks due to premature labor. One can watch only so many TV talk shows, and the medicine I had to take in order to stop the contractions made it almost impossible to focus on words in a book. So reading was out. Then my mother brought over as many Doris Day movies as she could find, and I watched them over and over again. From *Move*

Over Darling with James Garner to *That Touch of Mink* starring Cary Grant, my days were filled with Doris Day and her wonderful movies until I finally welcomed Abby Leigh into this world. Afterward, I wrote a thank-you note to Doris. I just wanted to tell her how much her movies had meant to me during those long days of bed rest. I certainly never expected a response, but I got one. Doris Day sent me a lovely handwritten note telling me how much my note had touched her. Wow!

Certainly Doris Day didn't have to take time to thank me, but she did. I cherish that note. No, I'm not an obsessed fan. I keep the note because it reminds me to take time for other people. This world would be a much better place if we all operated by the Golden Rule: "Do unto others as you would have them do unto you."

Are you a diva? Or do you take time for other people? Remember the Golden Rule the next time you're in line at a fast-food restaurant and the little gal behind the counter gives you the wrong order. If you're more like a diva than a Doris Day, ask the Lord to help you become more like Him.

Bronzed Beauty

· ·

*Those who live according to the flesh have their minds
set on what the flesh desires; but those who live in accordance with
the Spirit have their minds set on what the Spirit desires.*
ROMANS 8:5 NIV

There's one thing about Texans: We love to be tan. Sun worshippers
can be found throughout the world, but there are a great many of
these bronzed beauties in the Lone Star State. It seems there is a
tanning salon on almost every corner. I'll admit, I love to be tan, too.
I'd much rather show off healthy, tan-looking legs instead of milky
white ones. How about you? Funny thing about tanning. . . While it
makes you look healthy, tanned skin is actually a sign of sun damage.

When your skin absorbs the sun's rays, those rays actually
damage the DNA in your skin's cells. This damage causes the cells to
become dysfunctional, according to Michele Grodberg, MD, who is
quoted in an article titled "Can You Reverse Sun Damage?" on msn.com.
And those dysfunctional cells behave improperly, resulting in a
reduction in the production of collagen and elastin, a thinning of
the top layer of skin, a halt in the skin's natural ability to slough
off its dead layers, and a rise in pigmentation. Ultimately, these

dysfunctional cells can become cancerous.

Even though we now know that sunbathing isn't good for us–and even though we know that skin cancer is the most prevalent cancer of all cancers–still, some women are willing to risk their health and even their lives to have that healthy-looking bronzed body. We will risk it all for a quick tanning fix. We want to look good now, even if it means we'll have to live with sun-damaged skin later.

Sin is the same way. The devil will make it seem very attractive to you right now, but ultimately, it leads to death. Sin will always take you further than you wanted to go, keep you longer than you wanted to stay, and cost you more than you were willing to pay. So don't go there! Don't compromise your faith for a quick sin fix. They call women who sunbathe "sun worshippers." But that's the wrong kind of sun worshipper. We need to be *Son* worshippers. We may not be bronzed, but we'll definitely be beautiful in Him!

Don't Settle

. . . .

I will bless you with a future filled with hope—
a future of success, not of suffering.
JEREMIAH 29:11 CEV

*I*n the movie *Monster-in-Law* starring Jane Fonda and Jennifer Lopez, JLo plays a single gal named Charlie. She's never had much luck in love, so she's skeptical of most men. Then she meets Dr. Wonderful at a party. She thinks he must be too good to be true, so she moves forward very cautiously.

When he brings her coffee at the beach one morning, she asks him, "Why should I go out with you?" He answers, "Because I'm different." Before he can say anything, she turns her back to him and asks, "Okay, then, what color are my eyes?" He doesn't even hesitate and answers, "They're brown at first glance. But upon further inspection, they have amber flecks in them. . .and when you look into the sunlight, they appear almost green. That's my favorite."

She turns to face him, smiling, and says, "I would have settled for *brown.*"

It was a cute bit of dialogue, but in reality, women are often prone to settling for less than the best. Somehow, we've been deceived into thinking we don't deserve the very best. This is especially true if you've ever been verbally or physically abused.

Bible teacher Joyce Meyer has often shared how she always felt that she didn't deserve happiness due to the abuse in her background. Eventually, she realized that was a lie of the devil and began seeking God's best in every area of her life. Today she is on the front lines for Jesus, bringing millions of people into the kingdom of God. But just think if she would have settled for less than God had for her.

So what are you settling for in your life? Have you given up on God's best? Or is there something in your past that makes you think you don't deserve happiness, love, wholeness, and a beautiful life? Listen, if you've accepted Jesus as your Lord and Savior, your slate is totally wiped clean. No matter what you've done or what someone else has done to you, you are valuable to God and He desires good things for you. He wants to give you beauty for ashes–what a deal!

If you've been settling for much less than what God has promised you in His Word, it's not too late. Start expecting God's beauty in your life. Ask Him to help you realize just how precious you are to Him. Once you know that truth, you'll never settle again!

Giving Birth

*"Do not fear what they fear,
and do not dread it."*
ISAIAH 8:12 NIV

go to any baby shower and sooner or later the birthing stories
start. Comparisons run the gamut from the most nervous husband
to the longest labor. I'm personally intrigued by the unusual places
infants choose to be born, giving little thought to their mothers'
inconvenience or modesty.

My aunt June birthed one of her children in the elevator on the
way up to the hospital delivery room. Pat's husband was adamant
that his wife not deliver their child in his new Cadillac. (They couldn't
make it to the hospital in time.) So Pat delivered their bundle of joy
on their kitchen table. Grace's story may top both Pat's and June's.

Grace and her husband, Bill, were "bush" missionaries in
Indonesia decades ago. Their second daughter was born in their
lodging with Bill as the delivering doctor. Bill wasn't a physician, a
nurse, an EMT, or a paramedic. There was no 911 in those days, least
of all in the jungle. But Bill "read up" on delivering a baby. When the
time came, he and Grace and their little newborn just did it.

What amazes me about these three women and their colorful stories is their lack of panic in their situations. Each one decided she would simply do what it had come time to do–push! June and Pat didn't plan their unorthodox deliveries, but Grace did. Most of us would fear delivering a child miles from any kind of medical help or facility. Our serenity is tied to the familiar–to the known standard of care. Grace's serenity was tied to her God. She was confident that she and her husband were doing what God had called them to do and here He had called them to do it. By the time her delivery date arrived, she had spent a lot of time in preparatory prayer. She was ready.

Grace is now in her nineties and has had many difficult moments in recent months. Bill's Alzheimer's has taken him from her in many ways. Grace's health fails, too. She had to have a leg amputated. As I talked with her one evening, she rubbed the leg that now ends at her knee.

"I never thought this would happen to. . . ," she started. She sniffed back her threatening tears and held up her head. "God is faithful. He's taking care of me. We'll get through this together." Grace has never been one to indulge in self-pity–not when she was delivering a baby in the jungle and not when she lost a limb. Her serenity is no secret. Her "LORD is a God who knows" (1 Samuel 2:3 NIV), and she is content.

What a Bargain!

*"For God so loved the world that he gave his one and only Son,
that whoever believes in him shall not perish but have eternal life."*
JOHN 3:16 NIV

$\mathcal{T}$here's something intoxicating about finding a great deal. Some call it thrilling. Some call it a shopping high. I call it pure happiness.

If you have never been to a yard sale, a consignment shop, or your town's Goodwill store, you are missing out. From designer scarves to eclectic furniture, you will find it all at these bargain meccas. What they say about bargain shopping is true: "One person's trash is another person's treasure."

I have found many treasures on bargain-hunting trips. Once I found a Louis Vuitton scarf for only ninety-nine cents. Another time, a Carole Little suit for three dollars. On another occasion, I came home with a Banana Republic leather jacket for only six dollars.

Those kinds of buys make you want to shout from the rooftop. But those bargains pale in comparison to the greatest bargain of all time–salvation.

God gave His only Son to die on the cross so that we could have eternal life. All we have to do is ask Him to forgive us of our sins and accept Him as our Lord and Savior. We receive eternal life, healing, peace, love, wisdom, prosperity, joy, and so much more–all free to us, since Jesus has paid the price for our sins! Now, that's a bargain really worth shouting from the rooftops!

Make sure you share the love of Jesus with all those you encounter. Tell them about the treasure you have found in Jesus, and encourage them to pray this prayer with you:

> *Dear Father, we thank You for sending Jesus to die on the cross for us. We thank You for loving us that much. Today we ask Him to forgive us of all our sins, and we accept Him as our Lord and Savior. We love You. Amen.*

Sharing Jesus with the world around you will bring much happiness to you, and it will bring much happiness to those who accept Him as their Lord and Savior. Don't be afraid to witness for the Lord. He will open doors for you to share your faith. Just be obedient to walk through them.

Becoming Beautifully Obedient

. . . .

"If you love me, show it by doing what I've told you."
JOHN 14:15 MSG

*M*ary, mother of Jesus, is the most well-known woman in the Bible. We all know the facts about her. Mary was from the line of King David. She was very young when she became engaged to Joseph. We also know that when the angel of the Lord came to Mary and told her that she would become pregnant, she asked, "How can this be? I am a virgin." After the angel of the Lord explained how the Holy Spirit could come upon her and make her pregnant, Mary never doubted or questioned anything else. Instead, Mary responded, "I am the Lord's servant, and I am willing to accept whatever he wants. May everything you have said come true."

Wow. That totally amazes me. Mary didn't say, "Well, Mr. Angel, I think that's great, but I am engaged and my future husband is not going to understand or believe this whole story about my pregnancy, so maybe this isn't such a good idea." No, Mary rejoiced over the news. She didn't worry about herself. She didn't care what others thought. She just wanted to be obedient to her God.

For years, Bible historians have asked the question: Why did God choose Mary to carry His Son? Why her? Maybe God chose Mary because she had such an obedient heart. The Bible says that man looks on the outward appearance while God looks on the heart. See, God knew that Mary would do all that He needed her to do. He knew that she loved Him that much. God saw Mary's beautiful, obedient heart and knew she would be the perfect woman to bring Jesus into the world.

I want to be more like Mary, don't you? I want God to trust me so much that He chooses me for assignments because He knows that I'll be obedient. I want my heart to be so beautiful before God that He can't wait to use me.

Obedience really is a beautiful thing. Conversely, disobedience is quite unattractive to God. Even delayed obedience is disobedience. God wants us to trust Him so much that when He asks us to do something, we do it—flat out. No questions. No wondering. No delayed response. Just obedience.

If you are struggling with obedience today, ask God to help you. Tell Him that you long to be His go-to gal. Determine to be obedient in the little things, and soon your heart will be beautifully obedient before God. And like Mary, you'll get big assignments, too!

A Little R & R

. . . .

*The LORD replied, "My Presence will go
with you, and I will give you rest."*
EXODUS 33:14 NIV

*R*ise before daylight, spend a few minutes with God, get the kids
up for school, pack their lunches, slurp down a glass of OJ while
showering, get dressed, brush your teeth, make sure the kids get on
the bus, put on a little mascara, do the nine-to-five thing, pick up the
dry cleaning, go to the grocery store, rush home and fix dinner, help
the kids with their homework, do a load of laundry, have at least one
meaningful conversation with your husband, look over your notes for
tomorrow's meeting, call your mother, watch the eleven o'clock news,
and collapse into bed.

Sound familiar?

If you're like most women, you only know one speed–full speed
ahead! There have been seasons in my life when I just wanted to
"jump ship" and swim for shore. Bottom line–we're too busy today.

God didn't intend for us to be so busy. Psalm 23:1–3 (NLT) says:
"The LORD is my shepherd; I have all that I need. He lets me rest in green
meadows; he leads me beside peaceful streams. He renews my strength."

So how long has it been since you've rested in green meadows? My guess is–too long! Pastor Joel Osteen of Lakewood Church in Houston, Texas, says that he has to have a few minutes in his recliner each day to simply meditate on the goodness of God. Without those minutes of just sitting before God, he feels out of balance.

Pastor Osteen is not alone. If we don't take time to just sit before God and meditate on His goodness and His promises, we might spin our wheels all day long. But you say, "I have my daily devotional time each morning. I read one chapter of the Bible and a devotional entry, and I pray for fifteen minutes. I'm doing fine!" My response is this: you are doing well! Those things are very important, but if your prayer life is like mine, you spend all fifteen minutes praying for everyone on your prayer list, thank God for loving you, and call it good. You rarely just sit in His presence and rest in Him.

We need that green meadow time. Make a conscious decision today to rest in Him. Find a few minutes to bask in His glory. Pencil in "green meadow" time in your daily planner and stick to it. God is waiting.

Be a Love Power Walker!

. . . .

Above all, clothe yourselves with love,
which binds us all together in perfect harmony.
COLOSSIANS 3:14 NLT

*T*here's nothing more attractive than love. I recently heard a pastor say, "Love leads people to Christ, not preaching." Wow. I never thought of it that way before, but it's really true. People today are so hungry for love, they're looking for it. And if you have the love of Jesus to offer, they'll want it!

Listen, sister, if your husband is not currently serving God, this is for you. He will be won over to Christ through your loving spirit, not your nagging nature. So if you're spending all of your time preaching at him, telling him that he needs to get his sorry self to church, that's not showing him love.

Instead of running all over town to every Bible study, spend some quality time with your husband, loving him and respecting him. You don't have to honor the sin in his life; you just have to honor him. Call things that are not as though they were—call your husband a wonderful man of God. Speak your desired result. Put on his favorite perfume and a little lip gloss, and give him a kiss on the neck. Speak sweetly to him. Love him. And watch him come around. Before long, he will be sitting next to you in the pew. How do I know this? Because the Word tells us that love never fails. Love changes the atmosphere. So if your love-walk is more of a love-crawl these days, you need to take a crash course. Here's your assignment: Read 1 Corinthians 13 every single day. Meditate on the different aspects of love, such as: "Love is patient. Love is kind. It does not envy. It does not boast. It is not proud," and ask God to develop each of those attributes in you.

Look for opportunities to share love with everyone around you—especially your spouse. Pretty soon you'll be a love power walker, sharing the love of Jesus with your family, friends, and a world that so desperately needs it. The more you walk in love, the higher your love-fitness level will become! Your love will make the God in you so attractive, people will be curious about you. They'll want to know what makes you different—what makes you stand out in a crowd. And you can share the answer—Jesus! Just as you should never step out without putting on your lipstick, you should never step out without love.

No More Bug Juice

. . . .

But the Holy Spirit produces this kind of fruit in our lives:
love, joy, peace, patience, kindness, goodness,
faithfulness, gentleness, and self-control.
GALATIANS 5:22–23 NLT

*A*ll of the gals in our Bible study have a secret saying we use to keep each other in line. When one of us starts acting ugly, a loving sister in Christ will whisper, "Bug juice." The meaning behind it? Well, when you squash a bug, what comes out? Bug juice! And believe me, it ain't pretty!

In other words, when we're under pressure, whatever is on the inside of us is what will come out. If it's bug juice, that's what spews out. If it's love, joy, peace, patience, kindness, goodness, faithfulness, gentleness, and self-control–that's what comes out. That's why we need to spend much time in the Word of God, filling ourselves with more of Jesus and His promises.

Not long ago, my friend Susan was able to put this "bug juice" principle to the test when her daughter, Schalen, was in a very serious automobile accident. When Schalen was admitted to intensive care with a broken neck and blood clots on the brain–panic filled the waiting room. The situation looked very bleak. As the doctors shared the severity of Schalen's injuries with the family, Susan stood strong. Through tears, she declared, "I will not fear. God is in control. Schalen is healed in Jesus' name!"

When the pressure of the situation pressed heavy upon Susan, no bug juice oozed out. The only thing coming out of Susan was faith-filled words. She quoted scriptures and praised God for Schalen's whole and strong body.

Susan's positive attitude and faith-filled statements changed the entire atmosphere of that waiting room. In less than twenty-four hours, Schalen rounded the corner. In forty-eight hours, they had her up and walking. Only a week later, Schalen walked across the stage at Indiana's Bedford North Lawrence High School to accept her diploma.

Maybe you are in a high-pressure situation right now, and bug juice is about to blow! Ask God to develop the fruit of the Spirit on the inside of you. Spend some time today in God's Word. Meditate on His promises, and rest in Him. Pretty soon, bug juice will be a thing of the past and only beautiful love and faith will flow out of you. You'll emanate Jesus' love when the pressure is on. And like Susan, you'll change the atmosphere around you. There's already enough bug juice out there. Why not fill your world with beauty today?

God Has Confidence in You

He delivered me from my strong enemy, and from them which hated me: for they were too strong for me. They prevented me in the day of my calamity: but the LORD was my stay. He brought me forth also into a large place; he delivered me, because he delighted in me.

PSALM 18:17–19 KJV

How many times have your prayers been answered? How many times has God taken care of you? Your friends and family? What stressful situations have you passed through, trusting God to guide and protect you? How many times has it "worked out," when others thought it would not?

Perhaps you can think of an occasion when you trusted God to move actively in your life, the saving of a dear friend from disease, or perhaps a loved one's safe return home during a time of war, despite a life-threatening injury. Maybe it was during a difficult period in your youth, when confusion about where you "fit in" led to some ill-made choices for your life. At some point in our lives, our obstacles, our "calamities," may prevent us from living a godly life, from following the true path God has ordained for us. And, yes, we may find it terrifying to acknowledge that we are overwhelmed.

Yet, if we trust in the Lord and give our lives over to Him, we can clearly see that "He brought me forth also into a large place; he delivered me, because he delighted in me" (Psalm 18:19 KJV).

Think about that! He delights in us! By believing in God's grace and love, by trusting Him in the face of any and all situations, we find confidence to deal with our troubles out of the infinite hope, strength, and ultimately wisdom that come from loving the Lord. Nothing pleases God more than this, and by so doing we have acknowledged and allowed God's will and words into our hearts and minds. God knows your potential; He never gives up on you. He has confidence in the person you are right now and the person you can become.

The Skinny Wars
and Other Silly Competitions

. . . .

We won't dare compare ourselves with those who think
so much of themselves. But they are foolish
to compare themselves with themselves.
2 CORINTHIANS 10:12 CEV

I read an article about the "skinny wars" going on in Hollywood. It seems that female stars who appear on the same show are competing (either consciously or subconsciously) to see who can lose the most weight. To illustrate this Hollywood trend, the magazine showed pictures of Jennifer Aniston and Courtney Cox when they first began *Friends* in 1994 and how they looked a decade later. It was unbelievable. They'd shrunk three or four sizes. They had dropped from the 130s to 105 or so.

So are you in a skinny war, too? Maybe you're not trying to lose more weight than your female buddies, but are you competing against them in other ways? I'll admit, I am very competitive by nature, so I really struggle with this one. Chances are, you do, too. Women tend to get caught up in comparing and competing, and it never turns out well.

Competition can be healthy if it pushes you to do better in an area of your life, but if you're consumed with being better than someone else, that's not healthy. That's a wrong focus. You need to get your eyes off of that person and back on Jesus. The Word tells us that we are to fix our eyes on Jesus. See, if our eyes are fixed on Jesus, we won't be distracted by competition and unhealthy comparisons. Rather, we'll be focused on becoming more like Him, and that's a worthy goal.

Remember that God has a race all mapped out for you. You can't run somebody else's race. It won't ever feel right, and it won't bring you joy even if you win. You have to run the race that God has for you. It's your destiny. Don't waste time on the "skinny wars" of this world. Instead, focus on Jesus. You'll always be a winner if you do that!

Experiencing Happily Ever After

. . . .

So put on all the armor that God gives. Then when that evil day comes, you will be able to defend yourself. And when the battle is over, you will still be standing firm.
EPHESIANS 6:13 CEV

I love fairy tales. My daughters love fairy tales, too. Even the offbeat ones like *Shrek*. Have you ever noticed that in a fairy tale there's usually a damsel in distress? Typically, there is a beautiful princess who is held captive in a tower that is surrounded by a moat full of alligators and the occasional fire-breathing dragon. She waits in that tower, hoping that someday her prince will come. She dreams about the day a valiant knight on his white horse will ride up to the castle, slay the dragon, use the alligators as stepping-stones, climb up the tower, and rescue her.

Maybe you've had that dream yourself. Well, stop dreaming, sister! Your dream has already come true, and it's heavenly! Your Prince (the Prince of Peace) has already come on His white horse. He rescued you from that tower of sin more than two thousand years ago. And He didn't just rescue you. He also took away your victim status and made you into a victor! He turned you into an overcomer.

He even gave you armor—the full armor of God—to protect you as you fight evil and rescue others from that fire-breathing dragon—aka Satan.

Sure, fairy tales are fun to watch on the big screen, but I don't want to be a damsel in distress in real life. A princess—yes. A damsel in distress—no. God doesn't want you to be a damsel in distress, either. If you've been living with a victim's mentality for too long, it's time to wise up to the Word. God says that you are more than a conqueror through Christ Jesus. His Word says that you are highly favored. It says that God did not give you a spirit of fear. The Word says that we can use God's mighty weapons to knock down the devil's strongholds. Like evangelist Jesse Duplantis always says, "I read the back of the Book, and we win!"

Your damsel-in-distress days are behind you. You are a winner. You are a beautiful princess—a member of God's royal family. In *Beauty and the Beast*, you get to be Beauty. In *Cinderella*, you get to be the lovely Cinderella. In *Shrek*, you get to be. . .er, uh, Princess Fiona (when she isn't an ogre). And if you've made Jesus the Lord of your life, you are promised an eternity of "happily ever after." Now that's a story worth sharing!

God Rejoices in Your Confidence

*I rejoice therefore that I have
confidence in you in all things.*
2 CORINTHIANS 7:16 KJV

"But God wants you to have confidence!"

Those words echoed in my head as I tried not to hyperventilate.
Stage fright was making my palms sweat and my knees quiver.
Waiting to be introduced, I fought to stay calm, remembering those
words of support from a woman in my church. I loved Ann dearly,
and she had been a spiritual mentor and mother to me. When I'd been
invited to speak for the first time at a church, I had sought her out.

"I don't know if I can do this. Even the thought of standing in
front of all those people does all kinds of weird stuff to my body."

Ann laughed. "But this is a gift, an opportunity from God to give
your testimony, to tell those folks what He's done in your life. You
can't turn your back on that."

"What kind of testimony will it be if I make a fool out of myself?"

"You won't. Pray about it. He gave you the story, led you to
live it. He'll certainly give you the confidence to share it. Remember
what Paul wrote to the Corinthians, once they'd straightened

themselves out and were back on the right road. They'd gained confidence in their faith, and Paul rejoiced in that." She hugged me. "God wants you to be confident!"

I took another deep breath and let it out slowly as I heard the hostess winding up her introduction. "Okay, God," I whispered, "let's get me through this, and we'll both rejoice." I stepped up, thanked the hostess, and gripped the sides of the podium as if it were going to flee from the room. My voice trembled, but as my message began to flow, I relaxed.

God got me through it, of course, that day and many times since, mostly because Ann's words made an impact that has never lessened. God wants us to be confident—in our faith, in our gifts, and especially in Him, and He rejoices when our trust in Him gives us the confidence to tackle whatever challenge He puts before us.

The Most Beautiful Woman in the World

. . . .

They saw that his face was radiant. Then Moses would put the veil back over his face until he went in to speak with the LORD.
EXODUS 34:35 NIV

𝓕ilm legend Audrey Hepburn was named the most naturally beautiful woman of all time by a panel of experts in June 2004. Hepburn, the star of *Roman Holiday* and *Breakfast at Tiffany's*, topped the poll of beauty editors, makeup artists, fashion editors, model agencies, and fashion photographers who were asked to choose their top ten beauties from a list of one hundred.

The women were chosen for their "embodiment of natural beauty, healthy living, *beautiful on the inside and out*, with great skin and a natural glow to their personality, as well as their complexion." The article went on to say that Audrey Hepburn is the personification of natural beauty because "she has a rare charm and *inner beauty* that radiates when she smiles. Her skin looks fresh in all her films and her personality really shines through as someone warm and lively."

Wow, that's quite a tribute, huh? Wouldn't it be great to make the Top 100 Beautiful Women of All Time list—let alone be voted number one? But did you notice that Audrey Hepburn's inner beauty was mentioned twice in the judges' reasoning for choosing her? Sure, there were many other beauties that made the list–Marilyn Monroe, Cleopatra, et cetera. Some may have been even more beautiful than Hepburn, but apparently their inner beauty was found lacking, even though their exterior beauty was striking.

That's good news, isn't it? That means even if our skin isn't flawless, even if our teeth aren't perfectly straight, and even if our hair has more bad days than good ones, we can still "radiate beauty" because of our gorgeous inner looks. In other words, if your heart is filled with the love of Jesus, that is going to cause you to glow. Did you know that Moses had to cover his face after he had spent time in God's presence because his face actually glowed? It's true!

Spend some time with God today, and get a makeover by the Master. Soon you'll radiate His love, and people will find you attractive. You might even say, "You'll glow, girl!"

God Chooses You

. . . .

*Coming to Him as to a living stone, rejected indeed by men,
but chosen by God and precious, you also, as living stones,
are being built up a spiritual house, a holy priesthood, to offer
up spiritual sacrifices acceptable to God through Jesus Christ.*

1 PETER 2:4–5 NKJV

*B*orn only two years before the first women's rights convention in
1850, Mary Slessor gave the world a whole new meaning to the idea of
freedom for women.

Redheaded and bright-eyed, Mary knew even as a child that she
wanted to be a missionary. She felt God had chosen her to follow in
David Livingstone's footsteps, even though she had some growing up
to do first. When her family moved in 1859, she took a job in a jute
mill, working half a day, then going to school the other half. By the
age of fourteen, she was a skilled weaver who diligently continued her
studies.

At twenty-eight, she finally realized her dream and was assigned
to Calabar by the Foreign Mission Board. There she created quite
a stir by going against all the norms for women missionaries.
Abandoning her corsets and veils, she dressed in the style of the tribes

she worked with and learned to speak Efik, so that she could use humor and sarcasm in her confrontations with some tribal customs.

And confront she did! She had a great respect for the people among whom she lived, and they understood that. This respect gave her freedom to attack such practices as ritual killing of twins, who were thought to be conceived by devils. Mary convinced the tribal leaders that twins were a sign of male virility instead. She also worked for more dignity for women and battled the enslavement of girls and wives. One anecdote told of Mary Slessor was that she once came upon a group of men assaulting a young woman and attacked them so fiercely with her umbrella that they fled.

Mary's confidence to do God's will knew no bounds, and the local tribes in West Africa embraced her, calling her the "mother of all peoples." She continued to work deeper into the heart of the country, loving the people and bringing them messages of hope and freedom as well as the Word of God. She lived longer than many of her missionary colleagues, which some thought was due to her sheer will to survive. She succumbed to a fever in January 1915 at the age of sixty-six.

Mary Slessor, with her love of God and her determination to help people, stands as a model to prove exactly how much can be done when we have confidence in the God-chosen path for our lives.

Bulldog Faith

. . . .

And he did not do many miracles there
because of their lack of faith.
MATTHEW 13:58 NIV

*H*ave you ever heard the theory that people end up owning the dog breed that they most resemble in the looks department? Well, I'd have to say that is true when it comes to me. I am the proud "mama" to three long-haired miniature dachshunds. They have long noses and very short legs. Yeah, I would have to say that I share those same figure flaws. (You're checking out your dog right now, aren't you?)

But in the spiritual realm, we all need to resemble English bulldogs. Bible teacher Kate McVeigh once shared that Christians need to have bulldog faith. She said, "A bulldog only knows one thing. That bone is his, and he's taking it." And that bulldog won't let loose of that bone, no matter what. In fact, the English bulldog's jaw muscles are as strong as any athlete's muscles, and when it latches on to something, it really latches on.

Well, guess what? That's how we have to be when it comes to our faith. In Mark 11:23–24 (NIV), Jesus says, "Truly I tell you, if anyone says to this mountain, 'Go, throw yourself into the sea,' and does not doubt in their heart but believes that what they say will happen, it will be done for them. Therefore I tell you, whatever you ask for in prayer, believe that you have received it, and it will be yours."

In other words, you have to believe you have received your deliverance from drugs. You have to believe you have received your healing. You have to believe you've received a restored marriage. You have to believe that you've received your dream job. And then you can't be moved if it doesn't happen overnight. You have to get a locked jaw of faith on whatever it is you're trusting God to do in your life, and you can't turn loose until the desired result comes. So go ahead. Growl in the face of adversity and develop that bulldog faith. It may be a dog-eat-dog world out there, but with bulldog faith, you'll have a beautiful existence.

Peacocks of Happiness

* *

You, LORD God, have done many wonderful things,
and you have planned marvelous things for us. No one is like you!
I would never be able to tell all you have done.
PSALM 40:5 CEV

*H*urrying into the office one afternoon, I was totally focused on an upcoming meeting. I was going over some mental notes when, all of a sudden, I looked up to see the most beautiful sight. Next to the front door of our office building stood a brilliant blue peacock grooming himself in the sun. Rays of sunlight bounced off his fabulous feathers, making the sight even more breathtaking. I literally stopped in my high heels, for a moment experiencing total joy. I wanted to squeal like a little girl on Christmas morning. I just couldn't believe my eyes!

No, I hadn't been sniffing my pink highlighter. There really was a peacock outside, which I later learned belonged to a nearby rancher. This beautiful bird liked to roam, and on this particular day, he had roamed right into my life.

As I stopped to appreciate the peacock's beauty, I thanked God for reminding me of His presence in the midst of my day—showing me love and favor even when I'm caught up in the busyness of life.

The day had started like any other, but right in the middle of the mundane, God had dropped a peacock of happiness into my morning. While later contemplating my surprise visitation, I realized that God drops "peacocks of happiness" into our lives all the time. Unfortunately, we are often too busy or our hearts too hardened to notice.

You may never have a fantastic feathered friend show up outside your home or office, but be on the lookout for God's good work and loving-kindness toward you every day. Be mindful of Him all day long, and drink in those moments of pure joy. Maybe your peacock of happiness will come in the form of your child's laughter. Or maybe your peacock will be the lovely fragrance of a honeysuckle bush. However your peacocks come, take time to enjoy them, and praise the Lord for His blessing. God loves to surprise us with good things–especially when we appreciate the "peacocks" He sends into our lives.

Unconditional Love

. . . .

And now these three remain: faith, hope and love.
But the greatest of these is love.
1 CORINTHIANS 13:13 NIV

*D*o you love your family unconditionally? How about your friends? How about your coworkers? Okay, now for the tough question. You know that woman at church who gets on your very last nerve–do you love her unconditionally?

According to Colossians 2:2 (NKJV), as Christians our hearts are supposed to be "knit together in love"–agape love. Agape doesn't mean "I'll love you if. . ." Agape means "I'll love you regardless." That's the same way God loves us–in spite of all our flaws. We are to follow His example and love others unconditionally, too.

But agape love isn't an easy kind of love. It's the kind of love you have to work at all the time. That means you have to love your spouse even when he acts unlovely to you. That means you have to love your coworker even when she takes credit for something you've done. That means you have to love your teenager when he screams, "I hate you!" That means you have to love yourself even though your past is dotted with shameful events. You have to love all people all the time.

Sure, there will be times when everything in you will want to act less than lovely toward someone who has hurt you, but practice love anyway. When you release agape love into a situation, it's like releasing God. Talk about powerful! Once you begin practicing love, you'll become totally consumed with it. Pretty soon love will be your first instinct.

Bible teacher Billye Brim practices love in that manner. She once shared through tears how upset she was when a person verbally attacked her. But Billye wasn't upset about what was said to her. Instead, she was upset that those remarks had actually offended her, because that meant she wasn't walking in agape love. That's the kind of love-walk I desire. How about you?

Well, I've got good news. It's not out of our reach. Jesus wouldn't have commanded us to love one another if we weren't capable of doing so. Ask Him to fill you with agape love today. Make a decision to show unconditional love to everyone you encounter. Soon the world will look a lot better to you, and you'll look a lot better to everyone in your world.

Confidence to See Justice Done

· ·

Do what is good and run from evil so that you may live!
Then the LORD God of Heaven's Armies will be your helper,
just as you have claimed. Hate evil and love what is good;
turn your courts into true halls of justice.

AMOS 5:14–15 NLT

This passage of scripture literally changed two women's lives for the better.

For several years, Ellen watched a situation in her own neighborhood grow increasingly unjust. A man who lived a few doors down brought a wife, Angela, to America from another country, mostly for the purpose of having children. Uncertain of American ways and unable to speak English, this young woman relied on her husband for everything. He controlled the money and all her social contacts.

Ellen's first attempts at friendship with Angela were met with distrust and withdrawal. As the couple's children started school, however, they brought home school papers, from which Angela learned basic English. She read more magazines and, finally, returned Ellen's efforts at friendship. This open door, however, brought Ellen more grief when she realized the severe level of physical and emotional abuse the husband inflicted on his wife. She advised Angela to get help, but the young immigrant waited too long. The marriage exploded, landing the husband and wife in court. Angela, suddenly homeless, jobless, and still unable to speak a great deal of English, lost her beloved children because she could not adequately explain what had been happening in the home.

Like many of us, Ellen had been hesitant about how much to interfere in the personal business of another family. After seeking guidance through scripture and prayer, however, Ellen knew she had to speak up, not only for Angela but also for her children. Ellen and another friend stepped in and helped Angela find a lawyer, a place to live, and a job. They worked on improving Angela's English and wrote endless e-mails to the lawyer and the guardian ad litem who worked on the case.

Ellen opened her home for extended visits with the children and took detailed notes anytime they spoke of their father's abuse. "I couldn't let this go on and remain silent," Ellen said. "God simply spoke to my heart, and any hesitancy that I should help Angela fight for her children vanished."

Sometimes, even when we see an injustice, we don't think we have the skills or the strength to act. God, however, does have that strength, and He can provide the confidence and the wisdom to move forward.

You're Qualified

. . . .

*But Moses said to God, "Who am I, that I should go
to Pharaoh and bring the Israelites out of Egypt?"*
EXODUS 3:11 NIV

I recently read a bumper sticker that said, "God doesn't call the qualified; He qualifies the called."

That's good, isn't it?

In a world that demands qualifications for just about everything, isn't it nice that God demands only our willingness to serve Him? In fact, God calls imperfect people.

Look at Moses. God had a huge job for him in spite of the fact that Moses had killed an Egyptian, hid him in the sand, and then fled Egypt because he was afraid of what would happen to him.

Not exactly a glowing résumé, is it?

Besides that, Moses had a speech problem–yet God was asking him to approach Pharaoh and tell him to let God's people go free. Moses knew he wasn't qualified. In fact, he said to God, "Pardon your servant, Lord. I have never been eloquent, neither in the past nor since you have spoken to your servant. I am slow of speech and tongue" (Exodus 4:10 NIV).

But the Lord already knew that, and He still wanted Moses for the job. He said to Moses, "Who gave human beings their mouths? Who makes them deaf or mute? Who gives them sight or makes them blind? Is it not I, the LORD? Now go; I will help you speak and will teach you what to say" (Exodus 4:11–12 NIV). God already knew that Moses wasn't a gifted orator. He already knew all of Moses' shortcomings, but He still chose Moses to lead the people of Israel out of Egypt into the Promised Land.

Guess what? God knows all of your shortcomings, too–and He doesn't care. He wants to use you anyway. God doesn't need your qualifications or abilities. He just wants your willing heart and availability. He will take care of the rest.

So trust Him today and be encouraged. You are qualified in God's eyes. You can be excited and happy about your life because God has a plan and it's a good one (see Jeremiah 29:11). You may not feel qualified to do the things God has called you to do, but God is more than qualified–and He's got your back!

Give It to God

*"If you, then, though you are evil, know how to give good gifts
to your children, how much more will your Father
in heaven give good gifts to those who ask him!"*
MATTHEW 7:11 NIV

𝓘 love happy endings, don't you? That's why I love the story of
Hannah in the Bible. Hannah was a good wife to Elkanah, but she
couldn't bear any children. Back then, that was the worst possible
thing that could happen to a woman. In fact, a childless woman was
often divorced, or another wife was added to fulfill the childbearing
duties. Either way, the barren wife lived a bitter existence. Well, this
is what poor Hannah faced.

Even though Elkanah told Hannah that she was his best-loved
wife, Peninnah was the wife having all the babies. And to make
matters worse, Peninnah constantly taunted Hannah about her
inability to conceive. Can't you just imagine the tension in that
household?

Hannah became quite depressed over the situation, and she
prayed earnestly to God for a child of her own. Then she promised
God that if He gave her a son, she would consecrate him to the Lord's

service all of his life. God heard her prayer and she became pregnant with Samuel. You can imagine her delight. I bet she strutted her pregnant self in front of Peninnah every chance she got, don't you? But then it came time to follow through on her vow to God. After raising her only baby for several years, nursing him and loving him, she delivered Samuel to the house of the Lord, turning him over to Eli the priest. Hannah followed through and honored God because He had honored her. Don't you imagine that her heart ached as she journeyed home without her son?

But see, you can never outdo God. He loves to give blessings to His children. So God caused Hannah to become pregnant with several more children. She was no longer the barren wife of the house. God had changed all of that. God turned her unhappy life into a lovely situation.

We can learn much from Hannah's beautiful heart. She didn't take matters into her own hands and throttle Peninnah, although her flesh probably wanted to do just that. Instead, she cried out to God and trusted Him to meet her needs. That blesses God. He loves it when we come to Him as our Abba Father and say, "Daddy, we can't change this situation, but we know that You can. So we're trusting You to do so." And He will. Whatever you're struggling with today–give it to God. He has a beautiful happy ending waiting just for you!

Let Your Light Shine

. . . .

*"You're here to be light, bringing out the God-colors in the world.
God is not a secret to be kept. We're going public
with this, as public as a city on a hill."*
MATTHEW 5:14 MSG

Mary and her husband, Danny, own and operate the Bedford
Bible Bookstore in Bedford, Indiana. It is the place to go if you need
a wonderful gift item, VBS prizes for the kiddos, the latest Christian
music, or just about any inspirational book you can imagine. If Mary
doesn't have it, she can get it for you.

The Bedford Bible Bookstore has stood the test of time. Sure,
there's a Barnes & Noble store thirty minutes up the road, but there's
no Mary at Barnes & Noble. See, Mary doesn't just sell you products.
She listens to your concerns. She celebrates with you over answered
prayers. She points you toward the book that holds information
you've been seeking. She also offers hugs. Mary makes a difference.

In fact, would you believe that at one time, the Bedford Bible
Bookstore had sold more copies of *The Power of a Praying Wife* by
Stormie Omartian than any other Christian bookstore in the five
states that her sales representative services? And compared to many

of those bookstores, Danny and Mary's bookstore is much smaller. You see, that book so touched Mary's heart that she has shared it with thousands of women who have passed through the doors of the Bedford Bible Bookstore. Just think how many marriages have been enriched and possibly even saved because Mary pointed them toward Stormie's book. You might say Mary is letting her little light shine.

Mary may never know how many lives she's touched until she gets to heaven, but her willingness to let God use her has made a difference in thousands of lives. I know because I am one of them. So here's my question to you: are you letting your little light shine in your corner of the world? Mary didn't have to go to Africa to let her light shine. God is using her on her own mission field—Bedford, Indiana. Why not let your light shine where you live? You can make a big difference with your little light. So go ahead. Let it shine!

The Confidence to Have Unwavering Faith

. . . .

For she said to herself, "If only I may touch His garment,
I shall be made well." But Jesus turned around, and when
He saw her He said, "Be of good cheer, daughter; your faith has
made you well." And the woman was made well from that hour.
MATTHEW 9:24–22 NKJV

Twelve years. For twelve long years, this woman had bled, in more
ways than just physically. Her illness rendered her "unclean" by
Jewish standards, and her family and friends would have most likely
ostracized her. If she were married, her husband wouldn't be allowed
to touch her. The doctors she had sought out had taken her savings,
leaving her needy, hopeless, and desperate (see Luke 8:43).

Then she heard about Jesus. She heard about the healings He
had performed, knew that He spoke the word of God. Finally, there
was hope. If only she could get to Him! Taking a chance, she pushed
through the crowd, firmly believing that if she could touch the mere
hem of His garment, she could be healed.

Luke also wrote of this moment, saying that Jesus immediately
knew that power had gone out of Him, and He turned, saying, "Who
touched Me?" (Luke 8:45 NKJV). The disciples were astonished. With

all the people pushing and shoving at Him, how could He possibly distinguish one touch from another?

He knew, however, as did the woman, who was now terrified. She was unclean, and she had dared touch a rabbi. She fell to her knees before Him, trembling, as she explained why she had reached out to Him.

Jesus' response, however, was one of compassion and assurance. He was impressed with the simple clarity of her faith, and He comforted her and declared her healed.

Although Jewish society at the time did not always value women, Jesus did. He reached out to them, befriended and healed them, and honored them in His ministry. Nothing has changed; Jesus still cherishes each one of us.

Although trials and illness are a part of being human, our faith can remain strong in light of His love.

What's Your Trademark?

. . . .

*Take on an entirely new way of life—a God-fashioned life,
a life renewed from the inside and working itself into your conduct
as God accurately reproduces his character in you.*
EPHESIANS 4:23–24 MSG

$\mathcal{D}$o you have a signature piece of jewelry that you wear all the time?
Maybe an estate piece that's been in the family for a long time? Or how
about a certain perfume? Some women wear a "signature fragrance"
that really expresses who they are. My mother-in-law has worn Clinique
Aromatics Elixir for years. Every time I smell it somewhere, I think of
her because that's her signature fragrance.

I've never really had a signature anything. I pretty much just flow
in and out of whatever is "hot" this week and totally "not in" the
next. That doesn't leave much time to establish a trademark anything.
But one year I treated myself to a Mother's Day present—from me
to me. (Those are the best kind of gifts, don't you think? You always
ensure you get a gift, and you're guaranteed to get what you want.) I
bought myself a Tiffany & Co. sterling silver necklace with a matching
bracelet. I absolutely love it. It seems that almost every day I reach for
it. That set goes with most every outfit. Even though I love it, I don't

necessarily want to be known for it. I'd much rather be known for my Christian walk. How about you?

If we are truly living for the Lord, we should have a special way about us–something totally different from the world. We should have the fruits of the Spirit–love, joy, peace, patience, kindness, goodness, faithfulness, gentleness, and self-control–operating in our lives at such a level that people notice them. We should walk in such favor that folks expect for things to go our way. You might say we should wear our "Signature Jesus" every single day.

Just think–you might be the only glimpse of Jesus that some people ever see, so make sure you don't leave home without your Signature Jesus. Wear Him proudly–He's even better than Versace! He goes with everything. He's always in style. And He wants you to share Him with the world. In fact, He commanded it. So go ahead. Let the world see the Jesus in you!

What's Holding You Back?

. . . .

Thank you for making me so wonderfully complex!
Your workmanship is marvelous—and how well I know it.
<small>PSALM 139:14 NLT</small>

*F*anny Crosby, the author of more than nine thousand hymns and another one thousand secular poems and songs, never let her physical challenges stop the call she felt on her life. And she never let her disability become a hindrance in her relationship with God.

Born in 1820, Fanny had her vision at birth. But at six weeks, she suffered an eye inflammation. The family's usual doctor wasn't available, so they sought help from a man who claimed to be medically qualified to help. He put a poultice on Fanny's eyes, leaving the infant's eyes scarred. The "doctor" left town—and Fanny blind.

Growing up blind wasn't easy, but Fanny didn't blame God for her situation. She didn't ask, "Why me?" Instead, she determined in her heart to make a difference in this world. She expressed that desire in her first poem:

O what a happy soul am I!
Although I cannot see,

I am resolved that in this world,
Contented I will be.
How many blessings I enjoy,
That other people don't.
To weep and sigh because I'm blind,
I cannot and I won't!

When adversity happens in life, people respond in different ways. Some give up. Some get angry with God. And some become even more determined to reach their goals and dreams–like Fanny. Without her songs "Safe in the Arms of Jesus," "Pass Me Not, O Gentle Savior," "Blessed Assurance," and so many others, our world would not be the same.

So here's my question to you: What are you letting hold you back? If you've been dealing with a painful disability or if you've been emotionally crippled due to circumstances beyond your control, God cares. He knows you're hurting. But He wants to give you beauty for ashes. He wants you to know that His plans for you have been in existence since before the foundations of the earth. Despite your troubles, God's plan for you has never changed, and His plan is a good one!

If you don't know the plan that God has for you, ask Him to show you. Tell Him that you are ready to carry out all that He has for you to do. Like Fanny, you are an important part of His overall plan in this world. So go ahead. Walk in that plan.

You Can't Buy Happiness

* *

*This is how we know what love is: Jesus Christ laid down his life
for us. And we ought to lay down our lives for our brothers
and sisters. If anyone has material possessions and sees a brother
or sister in need but has no pity on them, how can the love of God
be in that person? Dear children, let us not love with words
or speech but with actions and in truth.*
1 John 3:16–18 NIV

According to an article in *USA Today*, you can't buy happiness—
no matter how rich you become. In fact, University of Illinois
psychologist Ed Diener was quoted in the story as saying,
"Materialism is toxic for happiness."

So, contrary to popular belief, buying an entire collection of
Jimmy Choo shoes will not make one happy. Now, I have to be
honest with you: I love to shop. When I walk into a department store,
my heart pounds with excitement. Sale racks full of designer clothing
beckon me. Flashy handbags and sterling silver jewelry seem to dance
under the store's fluorescent lighting, making a smile spread across
my face. I truly enjoy shopping, so when I read this article, a part of
me said, *Well, these people just don't know where to shop. I could show*

them happiness if they'd come to Dallas.

But, in reality, that kind of happiness is fleeting. Do you know why? Because true happiness doesn't come from acquiring things for oneself; true happiness comes from giving to others.

I am not saying that shopping is a bad thing. I am, however, saying that Jesus' words "It is more blessed to give than to receive" (Acts 20:35 NIV) are true. God created us to be givers because we are made in His image, and He is the greatest giver of all. He gave His one and only Son to die on a cross so that we could have eternal life with Him. As Christians, the desire to give should be strong in us, too.

If you have felt unfulfilled and less than happy lately, look at your own generosity. Have you become a taker more than a giver? When is the last time you looked forward to placing a tithe in the offering plate? Have you recently done anything totally unselfish for someone else? If it has been too long, then get back into the giving mode.

Call that frazzled single mom in your neighborhood and offer to watch her children for a while. Invite that widower in your church over for dinner and fellowship. Buy school supplies for an underprivileged child. And do it all unto the Lord. You will find that giving is the greatest high—even better than discovering Jimmy Choo shoes on sale!

The Confidence to Serve

· ·

In Joppa there was a follower named Tabitha. Her Greek name
was Dorcas, which means "deer." She was always doing good
things for people and had given much to the poor.
ACTS 9:36 CEV

𝒻rom the time that Jesus began His ministry through the travels
of His disciples, scripture is filled with people who came to them,
asking for healing. Dorcas, on the other hand, never seemed to ask for
anything, either from Peter or her friends. Instead, her heart was set on
serving, and one of her greatest gifts was the love she had for others.

Dorcas lived in Joppa, a beautiful seacoast town about thirty-
five miles from Jerusalem. Beautiful, but sometimes harsh, since
many of the men made a living on the sea. Losing a husband or son
was a frequent occurrence for the women there. Dorcas saw this and
responded to the need. Although she was a widow herself, Dorcas
didn't dwell in or on the past. She kept moving forward with her life,
"doing good things" and providing other widows and those in need
with clothes she had sewn herself.

Some Bible translations call her a "disciple," which is the only
time that this title is used for a woman. She may have served the local

church as a deaconess. No wonder, then, that when she suddenly fell ill and died, the believers in Joppa who adored her so much immediately sent for Peter. When he arrived, they were mourning her, but the widows grabbed him, showing Peter all the garments she'd made for them.

Peter was moved by their devotion, and he sent them away. Kneeling by her bed to pray, Peter called her name and said simply, "Arise." She did, and Peter took her out and presented her to the other widows. Before long, everyone in the area knew about her healing, which resulted in many of them coming to the Lord. All because Dorcas had the heart and confidence to serve others.

Being a servant is not easy. The work is hard and long. But when that work is done in the name of the Lord, even the simplest skill with a needle and thread can become a great tool for evangelism. Servanthood is a gift, and Dorcas clearly demonstrated that when we have the confidence to serve in small ways, great things can be the result.

Seeing Spots

· ·

*If we confess our sins to him, he is faithful and just
to forgive us our sins and to cleanse us from all wickedness.*
4 JOHN 1:9 NLT

𝑅emember the old exercise videos in which Jane Fonda would make
you do a million buttocks lifts and then say, "Now, go for the burn"?
Yeah, me, too. Then we progressed to *Buns of Steel*, *Abs of Steel*, and
any other body part of steel we could find. And how could we forget
the Thighmaster contraption? (I still like this one!)

Spot reducing has been around for a very long time. There's just
one problem with spot reducing–it doesn't work all by itself. In other
words, if you tighten and tone the muscles in your bum, but there
is still a whole lot of fat on top of that muscle, you're not going to
see the results you desire. That's why spot reducing never produces
the results you want if you don't also partake in some sort of cardio
activity to burn the fat. Think of it this way–if you have a six-pack for
abs but you have six inches of fat on top of the abdominal muscles, no
one will ever know you have a toned tummy.

Spot reducing in the spiritual realm doesn't work that well, either.
If you work on your anger problem but you leave those six inches of

unforgiveness untouched, it won't really make a difference. Or if you work hard memorizing scriptures in order to build your faith but you still have a layer of sin covering your heart, it's just a memorization activity.

Here's the good news. In the spiritual realm, you don't have to do cardio to get rid of those layers of sin. It's much easier. All you have to do is confess your sins and ask God to forgive you. The Word says He will! Then He will help you "spot reduce" until your spiritual life is as fit as Fonda. You don't have to go for the burn. You just have to go to God!

The Innocence of Youth

*Don't let anyone look down on you because you are young,
but set an example for the believers in speech,
in conduct, in love, in faith and in purity.*

1 TIMOTHY 4:12 NIV

$\mathcal{H}$annah is our sweet little neighbor. She may be only eight years old in the natural, but she is much older and wiser spiritually speaking. In fact, she's my role model. This is the last week of school here in Texas, and Hannah's second-grade class had its award ceremony yesterday.

Hannah is a very smart little girl, too. She won ribbons for making the straight-*A* honor roll, *A*'s all year, an accelerated reader ribbon, and several other awards, too. Hannah had worked hard to earn each one of those ribbons. She was proud of them. She was very happy–until she saw her best friend's sadness. See, Hannah's little friend hadn't earned as many ribbons, and she was pretty upset. Hannah gave her friend a big hug and said, "It's okay. You can have one of mine." With that, Hannah handed her friend the accelerated reader ribbon.

Hannah's mom, Stephanie, told me later, "I was proud of

Hannah for earning all of those academic ribbons, but nothing could've made me happier than when Hannah gave her reading ribbon to her friend." It was a selfless, loving act, and Hannah didn't think twice about doing it.

If only we could all be more like Hannah.

As children, we still believe the best in others. We still root for the underdog. We still care about others' feelings. But as we get older, we become jaded. We start acquiring that emotional baggage. We feel we must look out for number one or we'll never get ahead. Maybe that's why Jesus said the kingdom of heaven belongs to the children (Matthew 19:14).

Maybe it's time for you to get in touch with your inner child—the one who still believes the best in people. The one who has no emotional baggage. . .the one who isn't worried about number one. . . the one who gives up a prized possession just to make a friend feel better—the one who acts like Jesus. We all want to look younger, but we should all want to act younger, too! Follow Hannah's lead and become childlike today.

Expert Opinions—No Thanks!

. . . .

Then I heard a loud voice saying in heaven,
"Now salvation, and strength, and the kingdom of our God,
and the power of His Christ have come, for the accuser of our brethren,
who accused them before our God day and night, has been cast down."

REVELATION 12:10 NKJV

*A*ctress Debra Messing, who is known for her beauty, shared that she was always a little self-conscious about her looks, but after she became famous and sat in a makeup artist's chair every day, she said she learned she had more flaws than she'd ever realized. "The experts" were quick to point out her flaws and what they'd have to do to make her appear flawless. Talk about scary!

It's kind of like the reality show from several years ago called *Ambush Makeover.* Have you ever seen that show? You leave the house thinking you look pretty good, then suddenly you're ambushed by "an expert" who begins telling you that your hair is frizzy, your makeup is all wrong, and you look stupid in your ripped jeans. Ugh! Please don't sign me up for a show like that. (I think I'll go with the ignorance is bliss approach on this one!)

There's one thing for sure: The world is full of "experts" who will happily point out your flaws—even if you don't ask for their expert opinions. Sometimes those experts are in your family. You go to the annual family picnic and your aunt Lucy says, "Ooh, you've put on a lot of weight since last year. I read where you should drink more water to lose weight fast—can I get you a bottle of water, dear?" Or your best friend says, "I recently read about a new wrinkle cream that is guaranteed to diminish crow's-feet. I cut out the ad for you." Nice, huh? Oh yes, we love those expert opinions.

Yep, experts lurk around every corner. The devil even fancies himself as an expert. He loves to point out all of your flaws. The Bible says that he is an accuser of the brethren. In other words, he loves to tell you what a crudball you are, because if he can convince you that you're a crudball, he knows you'll never live out the beautiful life that God has planned for you. Like most of these so-called experts, the devil's opinion is worth about as much as the gum on the bottom of your shoe. Ignore him! You may not be perfect, but you're perfectly saved. You're perfectly loved by God. And if you've asked Jesus to be your Lord and Savior, your heart is flawless. So take that, devil! We're hot! And you just live where it's hot.

Where Are You Looking?

*"For My thoughts are not your thoughts, nor are your ways
My ways," says the LORD. "For as the heavens are higher than
the earth, so are My ways higher than your ways,
and My thoughts than your thoughts."*

ISAIAH 55:8–9 NKJV

$\mathcal{H}$elen Keller used to say, "When one door of happiness closes,
another opens; but often we look so long at the closed door that we do
not see the one which has opened for us."

Many of us have read the story of Helen Keller. She was born
a healthy, happy child in Tuscumbia, Alabama, on June 27, 1880.
But at the age of nineteen months, she suddenly lost her hearing and
vision as a result of illness–possibly scarlet fever. Her life was forever
changed. She was forced to grow up in a hearing and seeing world she
didn't understand, one that didn't always embrace her.

Her story is one of great persistence and triumph over adversity.
Beating overwhelming odds, this highly intelligent, sensitive woman
devoted her life to bettering those around her.

You might say she chose to look for the open doors.

Let me ask you this: Are you looking for the open doors in your life? When one door closes, do you stand there staring at it, longing to batter it down? Or do you trust God for another door of happiness?

The Word tells us that God's ways are higher than our ways and His thoughts are higher than our thoughts (Isaiah 55:9). In other words, He may close a door that you're sure is the only one that will ever lead to happiness. You may plead with Him, "Please! Open the door!" And all the while, He is trying to get your eyes back on Him so He can show you the even better door of happiness that He has waiting for you.

So don't waste any more time staring at the closed doors in your life. Get your eyes back on God and let Him show you that next door of happiness. It may be right in front of you.

Be Joyful, No Matter What!

· ·

Rejoice in the Lord always. I will say it again: Rejoice!
PHILIPPIANS 4:4 NIV

*I*n Paul's letter to the church at Philippi, he mentions joy or rejoicing more than a dozen times. What makes that so amazing is this: Paul was in prison when he wrote Philippians. And it wasn't just any old jail. Greek scholar Rick Renner studied the historic details of the prison where Paul was held and recently shared those findings with our church. It seems that this Roman prison was known as one of the worst in the entire empire.

The prison had actually been used as a septic pit for many years and over time had evolved into a lockup for the worst offenders. Prisoners were chained with their arms above their heads and forced to stand in human waste up to their hips. The prisoners had to stand at all times–no matter how weary they became. Since the prison had no windows or ventilation, the smell must have been horrid. In fact, many prisoners died from toxic fumes. Others died from rat bites and infection. Still others died from hopelessness.

The prison was that bad–so awful it sucked life itself out of many strong men.

So how could the great apostle write about rejoicing in the Lord? Paul had learned that the source of his joy had nothing to do with his environment or his physical state. He found his joy in Jesus Christ. It was God's own Son who enabled Paul to write: "Rejoice in the Lord always. I will say it again: Rejoice!"

Paul was surrounded by darkness, dung, and doom—but his heart was full of Jesus and joy. He fixed his eyes on eternal things. Paul knew that the Lord was with him in his suffering, and he knew that Jesus would deliver him from that place of despair.

So how is your joy level today? Take a lesson from the apostle Paul—rejoice no matter what! God is with you. He loves you, and He's completely aware of your situation. Don't be moved by your circumstances—even if you are waist-deep in debt, sickness, marital problems, physical addictions, or whatever. God is able to deliver you. So rejoice in the Lord always—again I say, rejoice!

Hello, Dolly

A cheerful heart is good medicine.
PROVERBS 17:22 NIV

I'm not offended by dumb blond jokes, because I'm not dumb. I also know I'm not blond." So quips country music star Dolly Parton. From the time she was a little girl, Dolly has known she is blessed in ways that have nothing to do with money. By her own admission, laughter brings as much joy to her life as the music she loves to write and sing. To read an interview of Dolly or hear her speak tells her listeners that this is one country gal who delights in having fun.

Back in the 1970s, Hunter Adams discovered a novel approach to the practice of medicine—laughter. Numerous studies have validated Dr. Adams's approach. Laughter lowers stress hormones and blood pressure. It increases the body's ability to fight disease, and it stimulates the body's natural painkillers. Yet thousands of years before Hunter "Patch" Adams and his Gesundheit! Institute were validated by medical literature, laughter's healing propensities were recorded in the biblical book of wisdom.

We can cushion much of life's hard stuff with a little laughter or cheer. Several proverbs attest to the transformation that comes from a serene and pleasant attitude. Such an attitude pushes its way from the inside out. "A happy heart makes the face cheerful" (Proverbs 15:13 NIV). "The cheerful heart has a continual feast" (Proverbs 15:15 NIV). "Joy fills hearts that are planning peace," Solomon tells us. And "an encouraging word cheers a person up" (Proverbs 12:20, 25 NLT). Inner peace can be contagious when we allow God to work a sense of contentment in us.

Of all the movies that have ever been made about the time the Lord Jesus walked among us as a man, The Visual Bible series offers the most refreshing portrayal of Christ. Why? It presents a Jesus who joins others in laughter–even uproarious laughter! Jesus loved children, attended celebrations, and spent time with a circle of friends known for storytelling and laughter: fishermen. Is there any reason to think He never enjoyed moments of unbridled hilarity?

A dynamite country music star, a doctor who uses laughter in his medical arsenal, and a King who knew that even kings need to kick back and indulge in an occasional belly laugh all give the same advice. It comes from experience. Find something to laugh (or at least grin) at. Let cheerfulness do its work. Let a smile bring some serenity into your life today–then spill it out on others.

Measuring Up—Even in the Morning

. . . .

*For we are God's masterpiece. He has created us anew in
Christ Jesus, so we can do the good things
he planned for us long ago.*
EPHESIANS 2:10 NLT

𝒟o you remember the first time your significant other saw you
looking less than lovely? I sure do. Jeff and I were high school
sweethearts, so he had only seen me at school and on weekends when
I looked my best. Then I became really ill and had to check into the
local hospital. Jeff and I had only been dating about four months
when all of this happened. Of course, he came to visit me in the
hospital, bearing balloons and flowers. And though I wanted to put
on a little lip gloss, I was too weak. I looked like death warmed over
when he came to see me. I remember thinking, *Well, if he still likes me
after seeing me that way, it must be love.* As it turns out, it was love!

But that was scary. I was so nervous for him to see me "all
natural," with every flaw exposed. Why are we so afraid of letting
down our guards? For many women, it comes down to one thing–
we're afraid we won't measure up. Even legendary film stars and
Hollywood hotties struggle with self-esteem issues. I once heard

gorgeous actress Cameron Diaz comment about her reality show, *Trippin'*, in which she nervously joked, "Oh, the pimples." The camera caught everything on film–even the less-than-perfect skin that Cameron was sporting in several of the episodes. See, even a "Charlie's Angel" gets a zit once in a while! We can't be glamorous all of the time.

So, aren't you glad that God loves us for who we are–the good, the bad, and the ugly? We can totally be ourselves with God. He knows us inside and out–after all, He made us! The Father sees you through eyes of love, and He thinks you're beautiful. You don't have to worry about impressing God. He already thinks you're great–even when you first get up in the morning. Now that's real love!

Just When You Think You've Arrived...

. . . .

I don't mean to say that I have already achieved these things
or that I have already reached perfection. But I press on to
possess that perfection for which Christ Jesus first possessed me.
PHILIPPIANS 3:12 NLT

*A*fter my father died, I did a bit of emotional eating. Okay, I did
a lot of emotional eating, which resulted in some weight gain. So I
turned to LA Weight Loss to help me gain control of my eating. I had
to relearn how to eat. After four months, I lost those ten pounds plus
another five–for a whopping fifteen-pound weight loss. I was thrilled,
and so were my weight-loss counselors.

Once I hit my weight-loss goal, I was put on the maintenance
program, which was a lot less restrictive than the original program.
I loved it! But I loved it a bit too much. I developed a false sense of
security and, little by little, those pounds found their way back onto
my scale. After about six pounds, I put myself back on the restrictive
program and lost those pounds again. I had learned a lesson–don't get
too confident or thrilled with what you've accomplished. Keep your eye
on the goal. (Oh, and don't keep mini Snickers bars in your purse.)

This same principle operates in the spiritual realm. I once heard

Bible teacher and TV host Paula White say, "If you ever think you've arrived spiritually, you're already in trouble." In other words, there's always more. There's always a deeper place with God. There's always more to learn from the Bible. Maybe that's why the Word says that pride comes before a fall. If you ever think you've arrived spiritually and quit pressing toward the goal, the devil is there to jerk that rug out from underneath your little feet. After that happens, the fall is sure to come. See, the enemy has only one goal—to kill, steal, and destroy. So if he sees an opening, he's taking it.

Don't give him that opening. Don't be fooled into a false sense of security. If the apostle Paul felt that he needed to keep pressing on, I'm sure that all of us have some more spiritual growing to do.

Never be satisfied with your walk with God. Keep desiring more of Him. Keep learning more from His Word. Listen to more teaching tapes. Spend more time meditating on His promises. Keep your eyes fixed on Jesus. Press on! You have much to gain, and it won't be weight.

Confidence to Pass on Your Faith

. . . .

I am reminded of your sincere faith, which first lived in your
grandmother Lois and in your mother Eunice and,
I am persuaded, now lives in you also.

2 TIMOTHY 1:5 NIV

*I*t's a truism we hear repeated all the time: Parents are the single
greatest influence on their children. Children watch and listen,
especially when they're young, absorbing the way their parents act
as well as listening to what they say. This is one reason that Lois and
Eunice have been recognized for passing on their "genuine faith," taking
care to teach Timothy the holy scriptures, an important step in leading
him to be "wise for salvation through faith" (2 Timothy 3:15 NIV).

Lois and Eunice were Jews, who had most likely been converted
by Paul when he stopped in Lystra during his first missionary journey.
Already grounded with a firm faith in the Lord, they accepted Christ
and continued to grow and practice their new faith with an unwavering
confidence. Timothy, because of the sound background his mother
and grandmother had given him, also accepted the call to Jesus,
becoming a second-generation leader in the new church.

Handing down our faith across the generations is a vital gift we can give our children, and the bonds across the years don't have to be blood alone. Many of the wisest people in our lives may be our spiritual kin and unrelated by genetics. Each generation has great gifts to share in wisdom, life experiences, and a deeper understanding of scripture that sometimes comes through walking with Christ for decades.

Mothers to daughters, grandmothers to granddaughters, mentors to the younger people in their spiritual care. We all can look at the beautiful lessons that Lois and Eunice passed on, and we can see the need and have the confidence to reach out to our own. Although we have no idea what kind of adults they will become, the teachings of the Lord will remain with them forever.

Get an Attitude Adjustment

*And the Lord–who is the Spirit–makes us more and more
like him as we are changed into his glorious image.*
2 CORINTHIANS 3:18 NLT

*H*ave you ever been to a chiropractor? Many people today are
turning to chiropractors for relief from pain and even for preventive
health care. I used to be a skeptic until I actually went to a chiropractor.
Wow! I had no idea the difference a little adjustment could make in my
life. With just one or two small adjustments–a crack here, a pop there–
my chiropractor put my hips back in alignment. Immediately, I felt
better. After just a few treatments, the before and after X-rays proved
what I already knew. I was better–a lot better.

It's the same way with God. He can make just one or two small
adjustments to your heart, and you will have a lot better attitude.
With an adjustment here (getting rid of jealousy) and a tweak there
(taking care of that anger), God can totally rework your heart. He will
fix things you didn't even know needed fixing–and before you know it,
your joy will return. You'll feel better than you have felt in years.

Of course, once you are back in alignment, you will need to go to
God for maintenance work–just as I have to return to the chiropractor

periodically to keep myself in alignment. God will constantly work on your heart to keep it in line with His Word and His plan for your life. That's how we maintain good spiritual health.

So how is your heart today? Are you out of whack and in need of an adjustment? If so, turn to the Great Physician. If you are struggling with worry, anger, unforgiveness, or anything else that isn't right, ask God to "give you an adjustment." He will! He wants to see you walking in perfect spiritual health. Go ahead. Get an attitude adjustment today!

Going It Alone

. . . .

"I am not alone, for my Father is with me."
JOHN 16:32 NIV

What can a woman who specializes in luxurious fabric have in common with a woman who's a time-management guru? What thread of similarity runs between a mother of twelve and a single missionary woman who travels and teaches the world over? At cursory glance, Lydia, Lillian, and Judy may appear to be as dissimilar as any three women can be.

Lydia lived in the first-century Middle East. As an enterprising businesswoman traveling across large tracts of land to peddle her exquisite fabrics, she became an early convert to Christianity. Accustomed to "taking the bull by the horns," she gave Paul the apostle and his companions a place to stay when they were preachers and when they were newly released prisoners. (See Acts 16 for her story.)

Lillian Gilbreth, the mother of a dozen children, became one of the world's first female efficiency experts. In the 1920s and beyond, she traveled all over the United States and overseas, presenting her husband's work (and her own) on smart business management.

Judy, without any family support, finished college and became a missionary working in Indonesia. For decades she taught children—only to retire and then continue to teach other adults how to teach even more children, even though she has never had any children of her own.

Each of these women sounds totally unlike the other two. Yet they share a common thread. In their couples-and family-oriented societies, each did it alone. There's no biblical record that Lydia was married. Lillian lost her husband to a heart attack at an early age. To this day, Judy remains single. "Going it alone" did not deter any of these women from what they were God-designed to do. Lillian and Judy both found contentment in doing what they were best equipped to do. That appears to be the case with Lydia, as well. She was not one to take no for an answer when she was in the position to help someone else (Acts 16:15). Being "women alone" did not stop any one of them.

Jesus knew He would be facing the greatest challenge of His life alone. He knew that everyone would desert Him. Like the Lord or any of the women above, we, too, can have peace in knowing we are ultimately never really alone. "Even if my father and mother abandon me," the Bible says, "the LORD will hold me close" (Psalm 27:10 NLT).

Clean Out Your Closet

· ·

*This means that anyone who belongs to Christ
has become a new person. The old life is gone;
a new life has begun!*
2 CORINTHIANS 5:17 NLT

Okay, I admit it. My closet is a mess. I have way too many clothes
and not enough closet space. And to be honest, there are many outfits
in there that I'll never wear again. Many women find themselves in
this dilemma. But not my friend Ally. Whenever she buys something
new, she simply gives away something else in her closet. (I am quite
thrilled with her system, because I have been the recipient of many of
her castoffs. From Chanel handbags to Nike workout wear, Ally gives
great stuff away.) That keeps her closet from becoming too crowded.

I have yet another friend named Dana who should be renamed
"Closet Organizer Extraordinaire." She organizes closets by season,
color, and occasion. It's amazing, really. Her rule is this: If you
haven't worn something in the past year, it goes. Like Ally, Dana gets
rid of something old and makes room for something new. This keeps
her color-coded closet from getting cluttered.

That principle works the same way in our spiritual lives. God is a God of order. Before we can put on new things, we have to do away with the old, outdated, and sinful things. If our spiritual lives are cluttered with things like lying, unforgiveness, unwholesome talk, bitterness, anger, or anything else that doesn't match God's attributes, we have to get rid of them to make room for more of God.

Your closet may not be cluttered with bad stuff. In fact, it might be totally jam-packed with good things, but if those things aren't what God has for you right now, they are clutter. They are as outdated as those parachute pants in the back of your closet. For instance, maybe heading up the vacation Bible school program at your church for the past five years was a very good thing. But if it was just for a season, and now God wants you to hand that duty off to someone else because He has a new thing for you to do, it's clutter!

How long has it been since you've cleaned out your spiritual closet? Have you been hanging on to things for far too long? If so, get rid of those things. Ask God to help you clean out your closet. He is the Master at organization, and He can't wait to see you wearing all of the new stuff He has for you!

God Rewards Confidence

. . . .

Do not throw away this confident trust in the Lord.
Remember the great reward it brings you! Patient endurance
is what you need now, so you will continue to do God's will.
Then you will receive all that he has promised.
HEBREWS 10:35-36 NLT

I just don't understand how you could go see that movie!"

I heard that a lot in 2004, the year *The Passion of the Christ* hit theaters all over the world. I have many friends who are not believers, and some refused to face the violent depiction of the crucifixion. I had all the negative reviews waved in my face. One friend who went with me couldn't handle the violence and walked out early.

It was definitely not an easy film to watch. Even harder to face was the knowledge that Christ had the power to stop what was happening to Him at any moment. The film became, for me, an extremely emotional reminder of what Christ endured to follow His Father's will. To save God's children. To save me.

Yet it also underscored that many of Christ's disciples also suffered in His name. Being a believer, a devout follower of Jesus, has never been simple or easy. Believers have been ridiculed, often persecuted, just for holding on to their faith. As I watched the trial of Jesus on the screen, I couldn't help remembering what the scriptures say about the persecution of disciples like Peter, Stephen, Paul, and others. Throughout history, men and women have been tortured and killed for pursuing a faith in Jesus, and today there are still places in the world where being a Christian can mean risking life and limb.

Even when there's freedom to worship, temptations lie around every corner—sometimes even from those who care about us. As a single woman, for instance, I'm often asked about my choice of chastity in the face of days of loneliness, and sometimes ridiculed for it. While they are not physically torturous or life threatening, such attitudes still test us and call our faith into question.

Sometimes I've wavered; I'm human. But my confidence to continue on this path, the journey all believers make, comes from knowing how much God suffered for me, how much He loves me and wants me to succeed, and the knowledge that the reward waiting at the end is more precious than I can imagine.

Knowledge Is Power

* *

My people are ruined because they don't know what's right or true.
HOSEA 4:6 MSG

Q: What do you call it when a blond dyes her hair brunette?
A: Artificial intelligence.

Entire websites are dedicated to dumb-blond jokes. Even though I'm not a natural blond (There, I said it!), I take blond jokes quite personally. No one wants to be thought of as an airhead or a clueless person. That's definitely not attractive. While it's fun to watch dumb blonds in movies and television sitcoms, in real life being dumb (whether you're blond, redheaded, or brunette) is not a laughing matter.

Oh sure, we all have our clueless moments from time to time. When you get older, they call them "senior moments." I guess before you qualify for senior discounts, they are called "blond moments." Whatever you want to call them, they happen. Most of the time they are harmless—like locking your keys in the car or momentarily forgetting the name of a friend or associate. These are simple lapses in memory—not a lack of knowledge. There's a difference.

The Old Testament prophet Hosea wrote that God's people were being destroyed by a lack of knowledge. In other words, what you don't know will hurt you. That's why we need to know God's Word. We need to understand our promises and covenant rights and walk in them every single day. God created us and then left us an owner's manual–the Bible. It's a road map for life. In it you'll discover the paths that lead to health, wholeness, peace, renewed strength, and a beautiful life. But if we don't take time to read it and memorize it and meditate on its words, then we will lack knowledge. Maybe that lack of knowledge won't cause physical death, but it might cause the death of a relationship or the loss of a job.

The world has taken this biblical principle and created the slogan "Knowledge is power." Maybe you've heard it before. Well, that's really true. When you have knowledge of God's Word, you will be empowered. Even your "blond moments" will be fewer and farther between. Wisdom is a beautiful thing, and there is wisdom in the Word–so get it!

Don't Be Moved!

. . . .

By the grace given me I say to every one of you:
Do not think of yourself more highly than you ought,
but rather think of yourself with sober judgment,
in accordance with the faith God has distributed to each of you.
ROMANS 12:3 NIV

Singer and actress Britney Spears was voted the sexiest woman in the world by a popular men's magazine in 2004. But in 2005, Spears didn't even make the Top 100 list! She went from being number one to disappearing from the list in one year. Did Spears suddenly lose her sex appeal? Did she lose her loveliness? No, on both counts. As it turns out, the only explanation is this—the world is fickle. People will love you one moment and passionately praise you, and the next moment they may lynch you. Crazy, isn't it?

That's why you can't be moved by what everyone else thinks. This is especially true when it comes to your outward appearance. One day you may get fifteen compliments on your new haircut, and the next day you'll get a zinger something like this: "Wow, you got your hair cut, huh? Don't worry. I had a bad haircut once. It will grow. Lucky for you, hats are in again this season."

Praise is a funny thing. While it's nice to receive, it can also destroy you if you let it deceive you into thinking too highly of yourself. Beautiful actress, television personality, and singer Jessica Simpson was quoted in a *Glamour* cover story as saying: "In this business, you're surrounded by people who praise you all day long. Even at the photo shoot for this cover people kept saying, 'You look so hot.' It's easy to turn into a diva and lose the qualities that made people like you in the first place. And I don't ever want to become that." (Pretty wise words from a person who didn't know if buffalo wings were chicken or if they really came from buffalo!)

So if you rely too heavily on what others think of you–especially what they think of your appearance–you'll never be consistently happy. People change. Their opinions change. But God never changes. He is the same yesterday, today, and forever. And He always thinks you're lovely. After all, He created you in His very likeness. It's like that old expression says, "God made me, and He doesn't make any junk." Hallelujah! Get in the Word of God and discover how God views you. Talk about a self-esteem boost! He adores you, and He always has–even when you wore the "mullet" back in the 1980s.

Don't be moved by praise or criticism. Just go to God and find your identity in Him.

Sweet Fragrances

. . . .

The LORD smelled the pleasing aroma and said in his heart:
"Never again will I curse the ground because of humans."
GENESIS 8:24 NIV

*F*ragrance is a powerful thing. Colognes, candles, flowers, and room fresheners attest to the popularity of sweet smells. If you want to sell your house, Realtors tell you to bake bread or boil orange peels and cinnamon on the stove before showings.

Some women (and men, I suspect) hunt for a cologne that becomes their signature fragrance. Simmering potpourri invites us to take a deep breath. One whiff of a past significant aroma can instantly transport us to a different time and place. A fresh bouquet of roses can bring a delighted "Mmmmm" to our lips—or a tickle and a sneeze to our noses. No doubt about it.

Fragrance smells and fragrance sells!

One of the first mentions of fragrance in the Bible follows the world's most devastating disaster of all time, the flood of Noah's day. Man's sin had become a stench in the nostrils of God Almighty. He decided to make an end of the rampant sin. Only Noah and his family escaped God's wrath. When the rain finally ceased and Noah and his family stepped on solid ground for the first time in months, Noah's first act was one of worship.

"So Noah came out, together with his sons and his wife and his sons' wives. . . . Then Noah built an altar to the LORD and. . .sacrificed burnt offerings on it" (Genesis 8:18, 20 NIV). From the sweet fragrance that found its way to the heavens came God's promise to maintain earth's cycle of seasons as long as the earth remains (v. 22).

Since we are made in God's image, fragrance can work powerfully in us, too. Lighting an aromatic candle may quiet us after a full day. Sinking into a bathtub filled with fragrant bubble bath may relax our tense muscles. Inhaling the satisfying smell of hazelnut coffee before taking a sip may soften our furrowed brow.

Sweet contentment through our olfactory sense–such simple delight!

Today you may be having the greatest time of your life. Your best friend may be having her worst. Since God calls us the "aroma of Christ" and an "aroma that brings life" (2 Corinthians 2:15–16 NIV), you may want to take your aromatic self to the side of your disconsolate friend. Maybe you can bring an hour of contentment to her just by being there. While you're at it, you may want to take along something that smells good. A sense of contentment may be as close as a pleasant whiff of flowers or a steaming cup of herbal tea.

A Weighty Issue

. . . .

"If any of you lacks wisdom, you should ask God,
who gives generously to all without finding fault,
and it will be given to you."
JAMES 4:5 NIV

*S*tanding in line at the supermarket, you can't help noticing the various women's magazines with headlines such as:

- Lose 10 Pounds in 10 Days!
- Walk Your Way to a Healthy Weight!
- Lose Those Last Five Pounds Eating Tofu!

If you're like me, you probably buy several of those magazines each month and try eating tofu for a few days until you give in and have a package of M&Ms.

With each decade, managing your weight becomes more difficult. Our metabolisms slow down if we're not working out regularly, and the weight slowly acquires on our midsections, hips, and thighs. Ugh!

If your "fat jeans" fit perfectly today, then you're not alone. According to the American Obesity Organization, more than half of adult U.S. women are overweight, and more than one-third are obese.

Obviously, we have some work to do in this area. But here's the good news: we don't have to do that work alone.

God cares about every little thing that affects our lives–including those extra five, ten, or twenty pounds that are hanging on for dear life! Let Him help you to achieve your ideal weight. Ask Him to get involved in your quest for fitness and a healthy lifestyle.

My pastor's wife had struggled with her weight off and on for years, and then she finally got a plan. No, it wasn't Weight Watchers, LA Weight Loss, or Jenny Craig. It was God's plan! She said that she prayed about her weight issue, and God impressed upon her to do three things: Drink more water than soft drinks; quit eating after 6:00 p.m.; and walk two miles three days a week. Those instructions didn't seem that hard, so she started following them. Twenty pounds lighter now, she is a happier, healthier woman.

The plan God gave my pastor's wife may not be a perfect plan for you, but rest assured, God has a weight-loss plan with your name on it. Just ask for His wisdom today, and leave those supermarket magazines on the racks. Who likes tofu, anyway?

She Can Cook, Too

*But the Lord said to her, "My dear Martha,
you are worried and upset over all these details!
There is only one thing worth being concerned about."*
LUKE 10:41–42 NLT

*C*all Sarah the superwoman. She can do it all. She has done every
kind of nursing there is–office, hospital, psychiatric, end-of-life care,
management. She's a mom, a Bible study leader, and a hostess who
always comes through. She's been a deaconess and a church camp
nurse and counselor. If all that isn't enough, she can cook, too.

Sarah makes dynamite meals for small groups–or gatherings of
a hundred. In the kitchen she mixes, stirs, bakes, and orders others
about with the kindness of a loving mom and the precision of a drill
sergeant. When a church wants to host a large event and feed a group
of hungry people, Sarah gets called because Sarah delivers.

Most amazing of all, Sarah is content doing this sort of thing.
She loves the role of hostess and cook. Whipping together special
desserts for company or adapting a recipe for six to feed sixty gives
Sarah a rush. She is serenely content doing what she does best in the
kitchen–cooking and serving others.

But Sarah is no Martha, distracted sister of Mary. Sarah knows how to leave off the preparations and the food when there's serious work to be done. The work of prayer and spending time with God never takes a backseat to her culinary talents. Sarah is as quick and eager to "hunker down" and pray as she is to wield a spatula–even more so. Like Martha's sister, Sarah knows "there is only one thing worth being concerned about" (Luke 10:42 NLT). Sarah knows how to sit at the feet of her Savior to listen and learn. Her serenity at His feet gives her serenity to do the tasks she loves on her own feet.

The Lord Jesus is not insensitive to those who find a measure of solace playing the role of hostess. He healed Peter's mother-in-law, who immediately went from her sickbed to waiting on those who had gathered in her home (Mark 1:30–31). A secret to serenity in doing comes with serenity's secret in being.

"One thing I ask from the LORD, this only do I seek. . .to gaze on the beauty of the LORD and to seek him in his temple. For in the day of trouble he will keep me safe in his dwelling" (Psalm 27:4–5 NIV). Even when there are ten for dinner instead of six, our time at the Savior's feet is where serenity begins.

Distinction

• •

Then those who feared the LORD talked with
each other, and the LORD listened and heard.
MALACHI 3:16 NIV

*W*e have a small circle of friends with whom we used to get together regularly for Bible study. We all took turns hosting the group and developed a love for one another and a deeper love for God and His Word in our times together. The years have brought change, however, and things are not as they used to be. The addition of children, changes of location, church affiliation, and even death have all worked to fracture our once tight-knit group.

But every once in a while—maybe every other Christmas, or once on a rare summer afternoon—someone takes the initiative and calls the members of this former home group together. Do you know what happens then? We pick up where we left off. There are no awkward moments. There is no "testing of the waters" or "walking on eggshells" until we feel comfortable with each other again. We just jump in and enjoy sharing with one another again. Laughing, talking, joking, and especially reveling in our common bond as Christians.

We talk about Jesus, about what we're studying in the Bible, and about sporting events and weddings and hard times equally. Our connection is deep; it's spiritual. We are comfortable in one another's company—because there's an unseen Other with us. In the verse above, God says when people who are His come together, He overhears their conversation and is pleased. Isn't it amazing that God looks to bless us in the simple act of meeting with others of "like precious faith" (2 Peter 1:1 KJV) when we delight together in Him?

Jesus said, "Where two or three gather in my name, there am I with them" (Matthew 18:20 NIV). Centered in Jesus Christ, our getting together with others to share about God's goodness brings more than a feeling of peace. It brings a promise. God says, "And you will again see the distinction between the righteous and the wicked, between those who serve God and those who do not" (Malachi 3:18 NIV). Service to God brings serenity and distinction. Not because of any innate goodness on our part, but because of His graciousness—and His fatherly approval of those who find their center in Him.

"You Look Mahvelous!"

• •

Thank you for making me so wonderfully complex!
Your workmanship is marvelous—and how well I know it.
PSALM 139:14 NLT

I have a friend named Mary whose very favorite saying is "You look mahvelous!" This gal knows how to give a compliment. No one can say it quite like Mary. You may not know Mary, but I bet you remember the character Billy Crystal made famous on *Saturday Night Live* by saying, "You look mahvelous!" (In the 1980s, he even had a song titled "You Look Mahvelous!" that played on radio across the United States.)

I've always loved that saying. It's better than just saying, "Hey, you look all right." It's much more exciting to hear, "You look mahvelous!"

After fourteen years of marriage, my husband knows which answers will get him into trouble. For instance, if I ask, "Does this outfit make me look fat?" his answer had better be "No. Are you kidding? How could anything ever make you look fat?" And if I ask, "How do I look?" he'd better not say, "You look okay" or "You look fine." Why? Because "okay" and "fine" translate into "adequate" or "You'll do." No woman wants to feel like she's just "okay." Women want to look and feel marvelous, right?

Well, in the real world, we often don't feel like we look marvelous. In fact, we may not feel like we even measure up to okay or fine. Am I right? Maybe you were raised in a home where praise was rarely given, so you're not used to hearing compliments. Or maybe you're married to a person who doesn't know how to make you feel special with words. Or maybe you never feel like you look marvelous–no matter how many times you hear it.

I have good news for you. God thinks you're marvelous! He created you exactly how you are. So even if you hate your freckles or you wish you were taller, God thinks you're perfect. He adores you, and He wants you to find out just how much. Go to His Word and read how much He loves you. He tells you over and over again throughout the Bible. Spend some time with Him, and find out how marvelous God thinks you are today.

The Courage to Influence

. . . .

*One of them was Lydia, who was from the city of Thyatira and sold
expensive purple cloth. She was a worshipper of the Lord God,
and he made her willing to accept what Paul was saying.
Then after she and her family were baptized, she kept on
begging us, "If you think I really do have faith in the Lord,
come stay in my home." Finally, we accepted her invitation.*

ACTS 16:14–15 CEV

Lydia was a magnificent woman. Successful, intelligent, perceptive,
and persuasive, she is the prime example of how Christian
businesswomen have been influencing those around them since
the first days of the church. Originally from Thyatira, a city in the
western province of Asia Minor, Lydia had moved to Philippi, where
she made her living selling purple cloth, a luxurious fabric made from
the shells of a mollusk. This cloth was rare, expensive, and usually
bought only by the upper class. Because no husband or children are
mentioned and the household where she lived is referred to as hers,
many scholars think she was single or widowed at a young age.

When Paul met Lydia, she was already a worshipper of God–even
though she was a Gentile–and she had gathered at the river to worship

Him with other like-minded women. When she heard Paul preach about Jesus and His redeeming work, the Lord "opened her heart," and she became Paul's first European convert and thus the first Christian businesswoman.

Immediately, she wanted her entire household to be baptized and publicly insisted that Paul and Silas's team stay with her while they were in Philippi. Embracing her newfound faith with the same energy and determination as she did her business, Lydia opened her home as a gathering place for other believers (see Acts 16:40).

Apparently proud of her faith, Lydia was willing to do what she could to give Christians a home and a place to grow in Philippi. Although Lydia is mentioned only twice in scripture, her enthusiasm for the Lord is contagious, and with Lydia as a role model, we should not hesitate to influence others toward Christ, and we don't have to be wealthy entrepreneurs to do it. No matter what our role in life, the confidence to share our faith comes from the power of the message of Jesus Christ.

To Follow Those Who Teach Us

· ·

But Ruth replied, "Don't urge me to leave you or to turn back
from you. Where you go I will go, and where you stay I will stay.
Your people will be my people and your God my God.
RUTH 1:16 NIV

$\mathcal{R}$uth must have been frightened almost out of her mind. With the
loss of both her husband and brother-in-law, and the death of her father-
in-law years earlier, Ruth's future was shaky and uncertain at best.

Tradition said she should return to her parents' home, but Ruth
and her sister-in-law, Orpah, clustered around Naomi, the grieving
mother of their husbands. Ruth didn't want to return to the house
of her father, but three widows alone had no way of supporting
themselves. Then Ruth's beloved mother-in-law, Naomi, decided
to return to Judah. During her short marriage, Ruth had grown to
admire and cherish the older woman, watching how she had nurtured
her family and worshipped her God. Naomi had family in Judah who
could take care of her, and as she prepared to make the move, Ruth
and Orpah faced a gut-wrenching decision.

Although Orpah loved Naomi, she apparently recognized the
wisdom in Naomi's advice, "Return home, my daughters. Why would

you come with me?" (Ruth 1:11 NIV). Ruth, however, had a dilemma that went far beyond financial and emotional support. Her closeness to Naomi, and the spiritual devotion of their home, had led Ruth to love the Lord. Thus, when she pledged her loyalty to Naomi, her words were not only of love for the woman and her people but for the God of all things (see Ruth 1:16). Ruth chose to trust God as well as the wisdom of Naomi. She placed herself in their care, and when Naomi gave her instructions on how to win the affection of Boaz, Ruth followed her guidance carefully. Her trust resulted in a secure home and family, and an honored place in the genealogy of Christ.

As women, we all benefit from the wisdom of our sisters in the faith, who can direct us and hold us accountable. Trusting God and choosing a wise mentor can help us as we learn more about our faith and develop a deeper and lasting relationship with our Lord.

Step into the Light

· ·

This is the verdict: Light has come into the world,
but people loved darkness instead of light
because their deeds were evil.
JOHN 3:19 NIV

*H*ave you ever been in a situation where you've had to do your makeup in a dim room? Sometimes when I travel, the lighting in the hotel room isn't so great. I put on my makeup as best I can, but when I get into the car and look at myself in the bright sunlight, I am horrified. Many times, I have on way too much blush or eye makeup, but because of the dark hotel room, I had no idea I looked like Bozo in drag. I thought I was looking pretty good, but the natural light told me differently.

Light is a powerful thing. It reveals much about us. This is also true in spiritual matters. The Bible says that Jesus is the Light of the World. When we look to Him and His Word, it also reveals much about us. Through His Word you may find areas of darkness in your life that you weren't even aware existed. The Lord may shine His light on bitterness that's been hiding in a dark corner of your heart. Or the Lord may shine His light on that unforgiveness you've been harboring for years.

If you've been living in darkness for some time, looking into the Light of the Word of God can be quite scary! You'll see many flaws in yourself. (You may find that you also look like Bozo in drag, spiritually speaking.) But don't run from Jesus and the Bible when you see your flaws and shortcomings. Instead, embrace the truth and ask Him to get rid of the flaws that He exposed.

God wants you to live free from that mess. That's why He has illuminated the situation for you. Finding out you have areas that need work is the first step to recovery, right? Let Jesus and His light fill you up and flow out of you. Continue to look into the Word and allow His light to reveal areas where you need growth. As you do this, you'll find that you are being transformed from Bozo to Beauty. Talk about an extreme makeover! Bring it on!

Get out of the Car

· ·

*"Now have come the salvation and the power and the
kingdom of our God, and the authority of his Messiah.
For the accuser of our brothers and sisters, who accuses
them before our God day and night, has been hurled down."*

REVELATION 12:10 NIV

$\mathcal{H}$ave you taken any guilt trips lately?

If you answered yes, then it's time to get out of the car. Guilt is not from God. The Bible tells us that the devil–not the Lord–is the accuser of God's children. God sent Jesus to die on the cross so that we could be free.

Free is free.

The freedom that Jesus bought includes freedom from eternal damnation; freedom from fear; freedom from lack; and freedom from condemnation and guilt. You don't have to take guilt trips if you have asked Jesus to be the Lord of your life.

But the devil will still try to lure you into his car and take you on a long, depressing road trip. He loves to remind you of all the mistakes you have made. He loves to tell you that God could never love you because you have been such a bad person. He is the chauffeur of all guilt trips, ready to take you on an extended drive whenever you will let him.

Don't let him. Just get out of the car!

Maybe you're saying, "But you don't know how badly I've messed up my life. I deserve guilt. I deserve to be unhappy."

If you really feel that way, then you have fallen for the devil's lies. I want to remind you of the truth: If you have asked Jesus to forgive your sins and be Lord over your life, you are guaranteed eternal life and His joy.

The next time the devil whispers in your ear, "You don't deserve happiness because you have done too many bad things in your life," boldly answer: "I am saved. Jesus wiped away all my sins and removed them as far as the east is from the west. He no longer remembers my sins, so why should I?"

That's what the Word says—and using the Word of God against the devil is your best defense. Just say no to guilt trips. Remind the devil that you are on the road to heaven—and he can't make that trip with you.

Bring on the Leg Warmers

· ·

Jesus Christ is the same yesterday
and today and forever.
HEBREWS 13:8 NIV

*A*hhh. . .the eighties. I remember them well. I graduated from
Bedford, Indiana's North Lawrence High School in 1987, so I am an
eighties lady. Oh yeah. I had hair so big I could hardly fit into my red
Fiero. I practically had to use a can of hair spray a day to keep those
big ol' bangs sky-high. I wore the neon-colored plastic bracelets up
my arms—just like Madonna. And I even had a pair of leg warmers.
Scary, huh?

Yeah, my daughters think my senior yearbook is pretty hilarious.

Even if you're not an eighties lady, I bet there were some fashion
fiascos from your time, too. For example, what was with that caked-
on baby-blue eye shadow of the seventies? Yuk! Fashion trends come
and go. One week, the fashion magazines say, "Long jackets are hip.
The longer the better. . ." and the next week, the fashion trend reads,
"Cropped, military-style jackets are the rage! Long coats are short on
fashion savvy. . ." Ugh! Let's face it. It's almost impossible to keep up
with the times.

Fads come and go. Styles change. And the way clothes fit our bodies definitely changes over time. (Can I hear an "Amen"?) Change is inevitable. From changing fashions to changing locations to changing diapers–as women, we're in the "changing" mode most of our lives. So in the midst of all this change, isn't it good to know that God never changes? Malachi 3:6 NIV says, "I the LORD do not change."

You can always count on the Lord. He's there through thick and thin, leg warmers and parachute pants, and everything in between. Let Him be the stability in your life. Run to God when you feel overwhelmed by the changes going on around you. If you'll stay grounded in Him, you'll always be "heavenly hip" and ready to face anything–even if spandex stirrup pants make a comeback!

Confidence in His Forgiving Love

. . . .

*Then, leaving her water jar, the woman went back to the town
and said to the people, "Come, see a man who told me everything
I ever did. Could this be the Messiah?" They came out of
the town and made their way toward him.*

Jᴏʜɴ 4:28–30 ɴɪᴠ

This woman of Samaria must have been shocked to her very core
when Jesus spoke to her. She expressed her surprise at His approach,
asking how He could dare talk to her (John 4:9). After all, she was
a woman, a Samaritan, and an outcast, which gave this Jewish rabbi
called Jesus three perfectly good reasons to turn His back on her. She
was used to being shunned.

The Samaritans, despite their estrangement from the Jews, were a
moral people who worshipped God (v. 20) and followed the law of the
Old Testament. She had broken that law by her immoral lifestyle, and
the fact that she was filling her water pot in the heat of the day clearly
indicated her avoidance of other people.

Women normally drew water for their homes first thing in
the morning or in the cool of the evening, and these were times of
community, sharing, and friendship. The other women of the town

would have resisted associating with her, and possibly even ridiculed her. Yet this man did not. He asked her for water–and about her life. He told her of His own living water, about a life without spiritual thirst. Jesus spoke bluntly to her about her past husbands, and revealed that he knew she now lived with a man she wasn't married to.

She may have been immoral, but this was one smart woman! She knew the scriptures, and she recognized Jesus as a prophet. When she spoke to Him about the coming Christ, He acknowledged that He was the One (v. 26). Wouldn't you be excited? She certainly was!

She immediately ran back into the city to spread the news. She didn't think about being ridiculed or avoided; she even forgot her water pot! She brought the whole city out to hear the news of the Messiah.

When Christ comes into our lives, whatever past sins may have clouded our lives are forgiven. Wiped clean. As with the Samaritan woman, He doesn't care what we were–only what we are going to be now that He is a part of us. We can start fresh, having the confidence to push forward and face whatever has been holding us back.

Be the Glue

A woman's family is held together by her wisdom,
but it can be destroyed by her foolishness.
Proverbs 14:1 CEV

Remember the old television commercial for Superglue featuring the construction worker? The man puts glue on the top of his hard hat and glues himself to a beam. Before the commercial is through, you see that construction worker holding on to his hat, his feet dangling beneath him, several feet off the ground. Of course, the goal of this commercial is to make you think, *Wow, that glue is really strong–maybe I should buy some of that.*

Superglue is really strong stuff. I have mistakenly glued my thumb and index finger together, and, wow, was it tough to separate them! Here's my challenge to you today: become like superglue for your family.

That may seem like a strange goal to you, but it's a worthy one. You should have God so big on the inside of you that His beautiful love, gorgeous goodness, and attractive acceptance emanate from you onto your family–sticking them together. In today's world, it's tough to keep a family intact. Divorce, even in the Christian community, is at an all-time high. Children run away from home. Family members turn their backs on one another. Let's face it: The Christian family is under attack. That's why it's so important to become the glue for your family.

So how do you become the superglue for your family? Live out the love of Jesus in your home. Let your family see your faith. Pray for each family member every single day. Speak peace over your household. Let God bond your family together with His supreme love, and get ready to experience a beautiful home life. Soon others will ask how you "keep it all together." They'll want to know why your family is different. And you'll be able to tell them about God's love and His peace and His goodness. Your words will stick in their minds, and pretty soon they'll be the glue for their families!

Sticking it out–especially when times are tough–is rare in today's world. But as Christians, we should set the example for a beautiful, happy home life. So be the glue today!

God Loves You—Flaws and All

. . . .

*So let's come near God with pure hearts
and a confidence that comes from having faith.*
HEBREWS 10:22 CEV

*I*f you listen closely, you can hear them. Women around the globe, groaning and moaning in dressing rooms. Are they in pain? Are they ill? No, it's just bathing-suit season, and they're trying to find the one perfect suit that doesn't make them look fat. It's a quest every woman embarks on, and it's one of the most daunting tasks she will ever face.

Seriously, is there anything more humbling than standing in front of a dressing-room mirror, under those unforgiving fluorescent lights, trying on bathing suit after bathing suit? I think not. I dread it every year. Because no matter how many miles you've logged in previous months, no matter how many crunches you've crunched, no matter how many desserts you've passed up, bathing suits show every imperfection.

While you might be able to hide a few dimples underneath blue jeans or a nice black dress, you're not hiding anything in a bathing suit. That's pretty much how it is with God. You might be able to fake-grin your way through church. You might be able to "play

Christian" in front of your friends and family. But when you enter the throne room, it's like wearing your bathing suit before God. You can't hide any imperfections from Him. He sees them all.

That truth used to horrify me—even more than trying on bathing suits—but not anymore. Here's the great thing about God. He gave us Jesus to take care of our sin, because God knew we'd be flawed. No matter how many good deeds we do, no matter how many chapters of the Bible we read each day, and no matter how many casseroles we bake for church functions, we can never be good enough for God. We can't earn our way into God's favor. All we have to do is ask Jesus to be the Lord of our lives, and we're "in." Then, whenever we enter the throne room, God sees us through "the Jesus filter," and all He sees is perfection.

If you haven't asked Jesus to take away your sin and be the Lord of your life, why not take care of that today? It's the most wonderful step you'll ever make. Now, if we could just figure out some kind of perfection filter for bathing suit season, life would be super.

What Was Her Secret?

. . . .

*"And who knows but that you have come to your
royal position for such a time as this?"*
ESTHER 4:14 NIV

❧

$\mathcal{H}$adassah's story makes for a great read, but living it probably gave
the young woman who became Queen Esther, wife of King Xerxes,
more than one stress headache and nervous stomach. Hadassah, a
Jewish girl also known as Esther, had been selected to replace Queen
Vashti. Vashti had refused her husband's request to parade herself
before his friends and associates. A search was made for an acceptable
replacement for Vashti, and Esther was taken from her home as the
"winner."

Esther transitions from simple Jewish girl to queen of Persia
and Media. She goes from rags to riches, from no cosmetics to a
full year of intensive spa treatments. (Check out Esther 2:12–14.)
Hardly a Cinderella story, but Esther lacks for nothing–except,
perhaps, a long life.

An adviser to the king persuades Xerxes to wipe out every Jew in
the empire. When Esther learns of the decree, through the cousin who
raised her, he gives her some chilling words. "Do not think that because

you are in the king's house you alone of all the Jews will escape" (Esther 4:13 NIV). If Esther had any composure left after being taken from her home and then relegated to a place in the harem apart from her initially doting (but now apparently indifferent) husband, this no doubt ended it.

Yet Esther presents herself in the account as a woman confidently–and possibly serenely–handling her impending doom with unhurried grace and that most womanly wile of all: willing submission to her man (see Esther 5:1–8). Esther may have been a bundle of nerves when she approached her king without his summons. Yet it's unlikely Xerxes would have welcomed a whimpering wife into his presence.

He knew and she knew that to go to the king without being asked meant her death–unless he extended his scepter to her. But even after Xerxes does just that, Esther carefully executes each step of her plan to prevent the promised genocide. Queen Esther successfully delivers her people from sure destruction. She once again gains the favor of her husband, the king. How she does it is recorded in chapters 5 through 9.

But the secret of her poise, the activity that preceded her actions, may surprise you. It's not so much what she does as what she doesn't do. Her secret is found in Esther 4:15–16. It's a secret worth investigating.

Drive Your Way to Happiness

Jesus answered, "It is written: 'Man shall not live on bread alone,
but on every word that comes from the mouth of God.'"
MATTHEW 4:4 NIV

Today's pace is insanely fast, isn't it? We go, go, go–all the time. We drive to and from work; to and from school; to and from the health club; to and from soccer practice, gymnastics class, dance class, (fill in the blank) class; to and from dental and doctor appointments; to and from the grocery store, dry cleaner, and other places of business; to and from our children's games and events; and on and on it continues. Sometimes I feel like I spend more time in my SUV than I do at home. Actually, if I added up the minutes, I probably do spend more time behind the wheel than at home.

From where I live in Fort Worth, everything is about twenty-five minutes away, so I'm forced to drive a large percentage of every single day. I used to sit in traffic and stress over things in my life. I'd drive like a maniac, trying to make my next appointment on time and occasionally bordering on road rage. I discovered that all that driving was literally driving me crazy, so I decided to make better use of the time.

Much to my tween-age daughters' disdain, I began turning off the car radio and tuning in to God. Sometimes I play praise and worship CDs. At other times I listen to teachings from my favorite preachers. Some days I listen to the Bible on CD. On still other days I use those minutes to commune with the Master. I pray out loud for everyone on my prayer list and spend time praising the Lord for everything good in my life.

Now, when I arrive at my destination, I'm not a stressed-out mess. Instead, I'm refueled with the love of God, fresh insights into His Word, and a renewed sense of happiness. I always joke that I have the most sanctified SUV in all of Texas. How sanctified is your vehicle? Some people call it "multitasking" when you accomplish more than one thing at a time. I just call it "keeping my sanity in the midst of a crazy, stressed-out life." Don't dread your drive time anymore. Instead, use that time to draw closer to God. Happy trails!

Deep Waters

· ·

"Put out into deep water, and let down the nets for a catch."
LUKE 5:4 NIV

*C*heri enjoys working in children's ministry, although experience has taught her that children's work is not for the fainthearted or the frail. Keeping up with the human equivalent of a perpetual-motion machine makes big demands on teachers and leaders. Besides the physical stamina and creative thinking that are required, the spiritual component of children's ministry dictates that the adult possess the greater spiritual maturity.

Cheri compares spiritual unpreparedness in ministry to white-water rafting. If we're in shallow water, dangers abound. Rocks, eddies, and rapids can spin our raft out of control. Smashing into a jutting rock can send us, with our helmeted heads, overboard before we have time to catch our breath. That's a good description of a spiritually shallow life. We find ourselves ill prepared for life's roughest waters. Only in a deepening connection with Christ can we be fit for our life's challenges, whether we're in children's ministry or not.

Cheri encourages those with whom she serves to deepen their

relationship with the Lord Jesus in order to meet the rigorous needs of ministry–and of life itself. Simon Peter and his partners had had an unsuccessful night fishing. When the Lord Jesus told Simon to go out into the deep water, the fisherman was skeptical. You can almost see the roll of his eyes and read his mind. (Been there, Jesus. Done that.)

But Simon obeyed and learned that launching into the deep with Jesus Christ makes all the difference. (It's all in Luke 5:4–11.) Simon Peter learned the lesson Cheri learned and teaches–going deeper with Jesus Christ prepares and equips us for more than we ever dreamed. "The Spirit searches all things, even the deep things of God" (1 Corinthians 2:10 NIV). The shallowness of praying on the run or speed-reading scripture in daily practice will not bring us into the place of spiritual maturity–or spiritual serenity. Are you ready? Let's paddle our dinghies and rafts into the calm waters of the deep, deep love of Jesus.

You're Got It All Wrong

And the servant of the Lord must not strive;
but be gentle unto all men, apt to teach, patient.
2 TIMOTHY 2:24 KJV

$\mathcal{P}$riscilla of the infant Christian church appears in four books of the New Testament. Her résumé, impressive even by today's standards, sounds like that of a contemporary woman. She and her husband had their own business, moved frequently, and had to adapt to life on the go—not always by choice (see Acts 18:2). They were teachers, hosts of house churches, and risk takers. Paul tells us they "laid down their own necks" to save his (Romans 16:4 KJV). Every sentence about Priscilla invites speculation about this fascinating woman. It's been suggested that since her name almost always precedes her husband's in the Bible, she was probably the more notable of the couple.

When an erudite man named Apollos came on the scene preaching about Jesus, Priscilla and her husband were there. "He was a learned man, with a thorough knowledge of the Scriptures. . . . He spoke with great fervor and taught about Jesus accurately, though he knew only the baptism of John" (Acts 18:24–25 NIV). With characteristic simplicity, Luke, the writer of Acts, sets the stage for some potential problems in this new organism called the Christian church. An unknown had come into the synagogue at Ephesus preaching "with great fervor" but telling only half the story. Do Priscilla and her husband get upset? Do they take this newbie to task? Do they get rattled and start to shout down the visiting teacher? Not according to the Word.

"When Priscilla and Aquila heard him, they invited him to their home and explained to him the way of God more adequately" (Acts 18:26).

No strong-arming; no heated, public exchange. Priscilla and Aquila heard their fellow believer out, gave him the benefit of the doubt, and then gently instructed him. They recognized their soul mate in the spread of the gospel–to the mutual benefit of all. (Check out the rest of Acts 18.)

What a demonstration of correcting a misguided, overzealous new Christian. Priscilla's calm serenity in sharing "the rest of the story" with Apollos is a lesson for all of us. More is accomplished with gentle instruction than badgering or embarrassing the less-informed or immature believer. Softening correction with genuine encouragement not only works in the church but also at work and in the home.

Makeup—Don't Leave Home without It

. . . .

*"The LORD does not look at the things people look at. People look at
the outward appearance, but the LORD looks at the heart."*
—1 SAMUEL 16:7 NIV

*M*y pastor leaned over the pulpit, smiled, and said, "I always tell
my wife to treat her makeup like the commercial says to treat your
American Express card—don't leave home without it!"

I glanced over at his wife and thought, Yep. *He is so sleeping on the
parsonage couch tonight.*

All teasing aside, the dog may be man's best friend, but mascara
is a woman's best bud. My mama always told me to put on a little
lipstick and some mascara at the very least, because you never know
who you might run into at the grocery store. She's right, of course.
The one time I headed to Walmart without a speck of makeup on,
I practically saw my entire high school graduating class. I wanted to
hide in the display of toilet paper until all the lights were dimmed
and I could bolt to my car. Ever been there?

Makeup is an amazing thing. It can hide blemishes. It can
enhance your eyes. It can make thin lips look luscious and moist.
It can transform stubby, faded eyelashes into long, curled, and dark

lashes. It can give your cheeks color, making you appear well rested when you've been up all night.

Makeup is a gift from God–I'm sure of it!

But wouldn't it be even better if our skin had no flaws to cover? Wouldn't it be better if our lips were already the perfect shade of pink? Wouldn't it be better if our cheeks were naturally rosy and our lashes naturally thick? If we were already perfect, we wouldn't need anything to cover our imperfections.

Well, maybe our outsides aren't perfect, but if you've asked Jesus to be your Lord and Savior, your heart is blemish-free. See, God didn't just cover our sins with His heavenly Father foundation. Instead, He sent Jesus to die for us and take away all of our sins. Isn't that good news? The moment we asked Jesus to forgive us, we became blemish-free on the inside. That's how God sees us–perfect and blemish-free.

The Word says that God looks on the heart, while man looks on the outward appearance. So while you might want to put a little paint on the barn before venturing out, your heart is already lovely.

Treasured

. . . .

But his mother treasured all these things in her heart.
LUKE 2:51 NIV

This is how the birth of Jesus the Messiah came about: His mother
Mary was pledged to be married to Joseph, but before they came
together, she was found to be pregnant through the Holy Spirit"
(Matthew 1:18 NIV). So begins our introduction to Mary, the mother
of God incarnate, the Lord Jesus Christ.

After her obvious question to the angel who brought the news
that she would birth the Messiah into the world, we read Mary's
unabashed statements: "I am the Lord's servant. . . . May your
word to me be fulfilled" (Luke 1:38 NIV). That, dear woman of God,
is serenity!

We are given only snapshots of Mary scattered throughout the
New Testament. Whenever we encounter this unique woman, an air
of serenity drapes itself around the scene. When she shares the news
of her miraculous pregnancy and the product of that pregnancy (the
Savior of the world), she sings. In her song she quotes passages from
the Old Testament books of Habakkuk, the Psalms, Exodus, and
Genesis (Luke 1:46–55). When shepherds heard about the Messiah's

birth and saw the infant Christ for themselves, they noised it about. Mary, however, "treasured up all these things and pondered them in her heart" (Luke 2:16–20 NIV).

Decades later, Mary saves a new groom embarrassment by referring the servants to her son for the provision of more wine at a wedding reception (John 2:1–10). At Jesus' death, and then again after His resurrection, she is a breath of shadowy calm at the horror of Christ's crucifixion and at the birth of the Christian church (John 19:25–26; Acts 1:14).

What was Mary's secret of serenity? Like the woman herself, the answer is tucked away in some unpretentious verses. She was "highly favored" of the Lord, who was with her (Luke 1:28 NIV). When we read her glorious song of praise to God later in the chapter, all her focus is centered in this One who is with her. "My soul glorifies the Lord," she says, "and my spirit rejoices in God my Savior. . . . The Mighty One has done great things for me. . . . His mercy extends to those who fear him. . . . He has performed mighty deeds with his arm" (Luke 1:46–47, 49–51 NIV). As a young girl visited by an angel or as a grown woman who watched her son die and return to life again, Mary never let go of the marvelous truth that brought her serenity: God has a mind full of those He loves (Luke 1:48; Psalm 8:4).

Don't Worry, Be Happy

. . . .

"Can worry make you live longer?"
MATTHEW 6:27 CEV

*R*emember that '80s song "Don't Worry, Be Happy"? (You're singing along right now, aren't you?) Well, it's not only a fun song with a great reggae beat, but it's also good advice. "Don't worry, be happy" is a good motto to adopt, because worry will steal your joy faster than you can say "leg warmers."

Worry is a sneaky thing. You might start the day just thinking about a situation in your life, but if you think too long, you will end up in full-out worry mode. You will start thinking things like, "If those layoffs really happen at our company, I don't know what we'll do. We just barely make it now. What if I can't get another job with health insurance? What if I don't get a severance package? What if? What if? What if?"

Don't let your thoughts take you there. If you cross over into the land of worry, you will eventually drive into the territory of fear and ultimately hit the city limits of despair. It's not worth it! Besides, no matter how much you worry, it doesn't change the situation one single bit, right? Prayer is what changes things.

Worry is not only a happiness stealer, it's a sin. The Bible instructs us not to worry. Matthew 6:34 NIV says, "Therefore do not worry about tomorrow, for tomorrow will worry about itself. Each day has enough trouble of its own."

That's pretty clear, isn't it?

Worry is a hard habit to break, especially if you have lived your whole life as a worrywart. But it's not impossible to overcome. How do I know? I was a world-class worrier for many years. I'd think about something for a while and eventually work myself into such a tizzy that I wanted to hide under the covers and eat bonbons all day. Ever been there?

If you have been taking regular trips to the land of worry, get off that highway. Take the prayer detour and stay on that road until you reach your final destination of peace, happiness, and victory. And while you're "in the car," pop in an '80s CD and sing along with "Don't Worry, Be Happy." Good tunes always make the journey more fun!

· ·

He [Apollos] began to speak boldly in the synagogue.
When Priscilla and Aquila heard him, they invited him to their
home and explained to him the way of God more adequately.
ACTS 18:26 NIV

*P*riscilla and her husband, Aquila, may have been the world's first husband and wife ministry team. They certainly set a standard for leadership, and Priscilla's equal partnership with Aquila stands as a reminder that God gives women ministerial gifts to use and reach others for Christ.

Priscilla and Aquila left Rome when the emperor Claudius expelled all the Jews. They settled in Corinth and established a tent-making business, working together. When Paul came to Corinth in AD 50, he stayed with them, working alongside them, since he, too, was a tentmaker by trade.

This gave them an extraordinary opportunity to learn the Gospel message, to question Paul, and to absorb the intricacies of Jesus' teachings. For the next eighteen months, the three of them worked to build the church in Corinth, and when Paul left, Priscilla and Aquila went with him as far as Ephesus. These two were very influential in Ephesus, remaining after Paul left in order to teach and build a foundation for the believers there. They ran a house church (see 1 Corinthians 16:19), and in one of the most profound examples of their work, they watched the dynamic speaker Apollos and recognized his gifts but also the errors in his message.

Instead of confronting him, however, they took him aside privately, offering him correction and encouragement (see Acts 18:26). Their goal was to strengthen the body of Christ, not humiliate someone making mistakes. They remained staunch friends with Paul, however, who continued to greet them in his letters even after they returned to Rome (see 2 Timothy 4:19).

Scholars have sometimes pointed to the fact that Priscilla is mentioned first and as often as Aquila as evidence that Paul sees them as partners, equal in strength. Larry Richards, in his in-depth book *Every Woman in the Bible*, reflects on the creation of woman in Genesis and suggests, "In Priscilla and Aquila we see the transformation of marriage and the restoration of God's original intent that married couples should be partners in all things in their life."

Without a doubt, Priscilla and Aquila helped transform the early church, despite exile, threat of death (see Romans 16:3-4), or the need to make a living. Women can still look to Priscilla to see that women definitely should have the confidence to minister to others when the need arises.

Looking for a Miracle

* * * * * * * * * * * * * * * * * * * *

You are the God who performs miracles;
you display your power among the peoples.
PSALM 77:14 NIV

I love to read beauty magazines. From *Glamour* to *Shape*, I read them all. But you know what I love reading even more than the wonderfully written articles? The advertisements. So many times you'll see ads saying things like, "Lose 30 pounds in 30 days!" or "Face-lift in a bottle." Oh, yeah, bring on the miracle-working products, right? We are hungry for miracles. We crave products that really work as much as we crave dark chocolate. We long to encounter something that brings results–not just in our beauty routines but also in our spiritual lives.

This week I saw the most amazing phenomenon on the evening news. A woman looked out her apartment window and believed she saw the face of Jesus forming on the glass. "If you look closely," she said, "you can see the outline of His face and hair. I saw it forming! I couldn't believe it!"

Word of the image soon spread throughout the area, and hundreds of cars started lining up in front of her home–just to catch a glimpse of the "Window Jesus." People began crying and worshipping

God right there in the front of a window. Why? Because people are hungry for a miracle. They are so hungry for a touch from God, they'll wait in line for hours in hopes of seeing the outline of Jesus' face on an apartment window.

Let me ask you something. How hungry are you for God? Do you crave His presence in your life? Or have you lost that passion for Him? If Jesus is no longer the first love in your life, spend some quality time with Him and His Word today. Ask Him to become first place in your life again, and thank Him for restoring that love on the inside of you.

Then determine to be the "Window Jesus" for others. If people are so hungry for the supernatural, miracle-working power of God–offer it to them! Don't be shy. They crave it! When you see someone crying in the supermarket, offer to pray with that person. Let Jesus shine through you. Be that window for Him. The world is hungry for what you have, so why not share it today? The world would be a lot more beautiful if we let His light shine through us everywhere we went. So shine on, and let the miracle-working love of Jesus flow out of you today!

Resistance Rocks!

My brethren, count it all joy when you fall into various trials,
knowing that the testing of your faith produces patience.
JAMES 4:2–3 NKJV

 $\mathcal{R}$esistance training brings results. I learned this when I first started doing some personal training back in the early nineties. I had always thought that lifting weights was reserved for the grunting, sweaty, bodybuilding kind of guys. I never dreamed that lifting weights could help women achieve the toned and lean bodies they desired. But the correct amount of repetitions and resistance can totally transform a woman's body in a very short amount of time. It's exciting!

Of course, it's not easy. Resistance training is tough. I've been known to grunt and moan and make faces in the weight room myself. It's hard work! Jeff, my husband, and I embarked on the Body for Life program three years ago. We felt really good at the end of those twelve weeks, and we looked a lot better, too! But those twelve weeks of disciplined workouts and a restricted eating program sure were difficult to get through. There were days when I dreaded getting out of bed in the morning because I knew my calves would ache the minute my feet hit the floor. Yep, we worked hard and saw results!

Resistance, whether in the natural or the spiritual realm, is never much fun, but it always produces change. During those stormy times in life–the times when you're in the valley and you're wondering if you'll ever see a mountaintop again–that's when the real growth occurs. That's when you become stretched. That's when you find out what you're made of. When you're going through the fire, that's when all of the chaff is burned away, leaving a beautiful, better version of you. So if you're going through some sort of resistance in life right now, don't fight it! Like James says, count it all joy! You're one step closer to revealing a new and improved you!

"Hopelessly Devoted"

. . . .

*Near the cross of Jesus stood his mother, his mother's sister,
Mary the wife of Clopas, and Mary Magdalene.*
JOHN 19:25 NIV

I grew up watching *Grease*, starring John Travolta and Olivia
Newton John. My favorite scene? I love it when Olivia Newton John
walks around the baby pool in the backyard in her nightgown singing
"Hopelessly Devoted to You." (You're singing along right now,
aren't you?) Of course, in that scene, she is singing of her character's
devotion to John Travolta's character–her summer love.

One source on Dictionary.com includes "commitment to
some purpose" and "religious zeal; willingness to serve God" in its
definition of devotion. But we can be devoted to many things–our
beauty routines, our workout schedules, our diet plans, our husbands,
our families, our churches, and so on.

Devotion can be a very noble character trait. You see glimpses of
devotion throughout the Bible–especially in the story of the cross.
Jesus was devoted to the Father–so much so that He was willing to die
a horrible death to fulfill God's salvation plan so that we could spend
eternity with Him. And though some of Jesus' followers dissociated

themselves from Jesus for fear of being crucified, too, the women didn't disown Him. It tells us in John 19:25 that Mary, the mother of Jesus; Jesus' aunt; Mary the wife of Clopas; and Mary Magdalene stayed at the foot of the cross, even though they were implicating themselves just by being there. They were devoted to Him. They loved Him more than they loved themselves. They were willing to stay with Him until the very end.

That is the kind of devotion that makes a difference in your life and in the lives of others. Let me ask you today: What are you truly devoted to? Your job? Your family? Your money? Are you so devoted to your workout routine that you give it priority over your morning devotional time? Or are you willing to spend time at the foot of the cross, just basking in His presence? That's what devotion is all about. You know what's so amazing about Jesus? The Word says if you seek Him, all of the other things will be added to you. It's a win-win situation!

Unlike the song's lyrics, you won't be "hopelessly devoted" when devoting your life to Jesus. Once you pledge your love and life to Jesus, you'll become "hopeful and devoted to Him." Jesus is all about hope. Your destiny lies in your devotion to Him. So go ahead and pledge your devotion to Jesus today. If you do, your life is guaranteed to be beautiful!

With Spit, Dirt, and a Hairpin

································

I lie awake; I have become like a bird alone on a roof.
PSALM 102:7 NIV

*L*ocked in separate cells, the missionary doctor and her physician husband found themselves in a Manchurian concentration camp. Days without change in routine or surroundings loomed before Dr. Byram. She didn't know how long she would be in her solitary cell. She didn't know if she'd emerge from it alive. All she had with her was her Bible.

Where can a woman find serenity while imprisoned in a foreign land without friend, family, or aid of any kind close at hand? Being used to busy days and nights of ministry and healing, how would she now pass these interminable hours alone? Could she find any serenity in this? Could she keep her sanity?

Dr. Byram opened her Bible and began reading. She decided to study the Word of God from cover to cover. She had no paper, no pen, no means readily at hand to record all her thoughts and insights to keep, should she ever get out of solitary confinement. She scratched her head and her finger touched something hard and straight. She withdrew the hairpin from her hair and studied it for a moment. She stuck the end of it in her mouth and then put the tip in the dust of her dirt floor. She pressed it to a page of her Bible. It worked!

Until she was released from prison, this woman penned the thoughts and reflections of her solitary Bible study with a hairpin, her saliva, and the dirt of her cell floor. She never forgot her time alone with God in that solitary cell. Meticulously recorded in her Bible, her solitary lessons were carefully inscribed on her soul, as well.

From that experience in Manchuria, Dr. Byram became a woman of prayer like few others. Once free from her imprisonment, she spent ninety minutes of every day for the rest of her life in prayer. She learned her secret of serenity (and prayer) in solitary confinement.

Sometimes we may feel as if we're in solitary confinement. Our health keeps us homebound, or friends and family have died or moved away. We may have more time alone–like a lone bird on a roof–than we wish. Can we do with those hours, days, weeks, and months what this missionary doctor did with hers?

Jesus has never made a promise He can't or won't keep. Those promises include, "Be sure of this: I am with you always, even to the end of the age" (Matthew 28:20 NLT).

Find Your Precedent

· · · · · · · · · · · · · · · · · · · ·

Elkanah made love to his wife Hannah, and the LORD
remembered her. So in the course of time Hannah became
pregnant and gave birth to a son. She named him Samuel,
saying, "Because I asked the LORD for him."
1 SAMUEL 1:19–20 NIV

𝒯he Bible is more than just a good book filled with great stories. It's
alive. It's pertinent. It's full of promises. It's our lifeline! So why do
so many of us leave it on the coffee table instead of discovering its
power and relevance today?

My oldest niece, Mandy, found out just how powerful and alive
the Word of God is when she began believing for a baby. She and her
husband, Chris, tried for several years to conceive, but every month
the pregnancy test came back negative. She was discouraged. Lots of
people gave her advice: "Take this vitamin, and it will help you get
pregnant"; "Try conceiving when there is a full moon"; "Stop eating
acidic food and you'll have a greater chance of success." Mandy
followed every bit of advice, trying desperately to become pregnant–
but the only thing she became was depressed.

Then her mother suggested, "Mandy, honey, why don't you find some scriptures to stand on? Find your promises in the Word of God and pray them over yourself every single day. The Word works!"

Mandy had been a Christian since she was a little girl, so she was certainly open to the suggestion. Since that was about the only thing she hadn't tried, Mandy was willing to give the Word a shot. She dug into the Bible and found the story of how Sarah had given birth to Isaac. Then she found the story of how Hannah had believed God for a baby and finally given birth to Samuel and several other children, too.

Mandy found a precedent in the Word of God and asked God to do for her what He had done for Sarah and Hannah. And He did! She stood on those scriptures for three months, and that's when her pregnancy test came back positive. Mandy gave birth to a healthy baby boy on February 15, 2006.

Jesus once told a story of an oppressed widow who pestered a judge until she got the justice she so desperately wanted. The moral of the story? According to Jesus, people "should always pray and not give up" (Luke 18:1 NIV).

Not every prayer will be answered the way we may hope. Even Jesus asked His Father if the trauma of the crucifixion could be avoided—but concluded His prayer with the words "yet not my will, but yours be done" (Luke 22:42 NIV).

God has promises for all of us—promises of an abundant life and of peace, hope, and joy. Those universal promises may also include personal blessings for our families, workplaces, and churches. So dust off that Bible and find what God says about your situation. The Word works all the time. Now, that's something to be happy about!

Happiness Is a Beautiful Thing

A happy heart makes the face cheerful. . . .
The cheerful heart has a continual feast.
PROVERBS 15:13, 15 NIV

My mother has always been a happy person. When I was growing up, Mom's happiness bugged me. It didn't matter if it was raining outside. It didn't matter if our air-conditioning went out in mid-July. It didn't matter if one of her friends talked ugly to her. Mom always chose happiness. She'd begin each day something like this. She'd burst into my bedroom, flip on my light switch, and begin her very loud rendition of "This is the day that the Lord has made. Let us rejoice and be glad in it." She'd sing at the top of her lungs and occasionally clap in time, as well. What a way to start the day, eh? There was no sleeping in at our house, because if you didn't get up, she'd just start another verse!

After my father passed away last year, I didn't hear my mom singing anymore. I worried about her. I prayed to God, "Please restore the song back into my mother's life." After a period of grieving, little by little, Mom's happiness began to return. It started with a hum, and now she's all-out singing again. I'm still waiting for that loud clapping to return, but I'm sure it's in the works. Why? Because Mom doesn't base her happiness on her circumstances. Sure, she's lonely without Daddy, but she chooses to be happy because of Jesus. She chooses to focus on the beauty in life–not the tragedy.

How is your happiness level? If it has been a while since you've burst forth in song, give it a whirl! Sing praises unto God until you sing yourself happy. But you say, "You don't know what I'm going through right now. There's no way I can be happy." You may be right. But through Jesus you can be happy. Job 8:21 NIV says, "He will yet fill your mouth with laughter and your lips with shouts of joy." That's a promise you can count on! He will–but you have to want it.

If you choose to be happy, you'll discover more people will want to be around you. Being happy simply makes you more attractive. Your happiness will be infectious. Happiness will become a lifelong habit, as it has been for my mom. You may even find yourself humming happily all day long. Beware: Loud clapping is soon to follow! Go ahead–choose happiness today! It's a beautiful life!

From an Ugly Duckling to a Beautiful Swan

"I will give you a new heart, and I will put a new spirit in you.
I will take out your stony, stubborn heart
and give you a tender, responsive heart."
EZEKIEL 36:26 NLT

$\mathcal{D}$id you ever watch the reality show called *The Swan*? It's amazing. The show selects plain-Jane women and some really homely gals, too, and through plastic surgery, cosmetic dentistry, lots of liposuction, personal training and diet modifications, hair color and extensions, microdermabrasion, and sometimes other minor surgeries, these women come out looking like supermodels. Then, at the end of the show, the finalists compete for "The Swan" beauty queen crown. Pretty wild, isn't it?

I watched the show in amazement the first two seasons, all the while deciding what I would ask to have altered, sucked, and tucked should I ever get the chance to be on a show like that. (I bet you did the same thing if you watched!) What was most interesting to me was when the "new and improved" women met with their families for the first time after their dramatic transformations. Sometimes the women looked so different, their babies didn't even know them! And their husbands couldn't stop staring at them. Talk about a makeover! These women weren't even recognizable. From their teeth to their toenails, they were totally improved in every way. Though there was some pain and suffering involved over their three-month transformation, the end result was beautifully astonishing.

Well, we may not be able to be featured on any television make-over shows, but we can have that same sort of life-altering makeover on the inside simply by letting the Master do His best work. The minute we receive Jesus as our Lord and Savior, He wipes the slate clean and gives us a new start. The Word says we actually become new creatures.

And that's not all! After our initial God experience, He continues making minor adjustments in our attitudes, and before long, we're hardly the same person. Our likes and dislikes change. The places we want to hang out change. The way we choose to take care of our bodies (the temple of the Holy Spirit) changes. Even our friend choices change. And over time, we leave that old, ugly duckling spirit behind and emerge a beautiful swan.

When you get a makeover by the Master, you will become more confident in who you are, and people will automatically be drawn to you. When you spend time with the Lord, you're like a people magnet. They won't know why they like you–they just will! You become more attractive. You smile more. You laugh more. You love more. Why not let the Master give you a makeover today? There's a beautiful swan in you just waiting to escape.

Confidence in Action

. . . .

When Abigail saw David, she quickly got off her donkey
and bowed down before David with her face to the ground.
She fell at his feet and said: "Pardon your servant, my lord,
and let me speak to you; hear what your servant has to say."

4 SAMUEL 25:23–24 NIV

$\mathcal{H}$ow many women have the confidence to believe they could stop an army? Abigail of Maon, married to Nabal, lived in a culture in which women had little social or legal power. Her own talents would have been focused on her home, not the court or the battlefield. Yet, while Abigail would have been seen as little more than the wife of a fool by her society, she was far from powerless.

Scripture describes her as intelligent and beautiful, and even her husband's servants relied on her wisdom when Nabal put the household at risk with his foolish pride. The reason was that Abigail had a secret weapon: God. Faced with the news that an angry David was leading an equally enraged army toward her home, she didn't hesitate.

Trusting in God's protection—and in her belief that David was indeed a man after God's own heart—she confronted the furious warrior and begged him to hear her. She appealed to his own belief in God's mercy and judgment, and she asked him to let God deal with Nabal.

Abigail had the intelligence and wisdom to know what to do, but her confidence to put her knowledge into action had only one source–the same source every believing woman can draw on. Standing on a mountain path, with only food-laden donkeys at her back, Abigail was at the complete mercy of David's rage. He could have killed her without question and gone on to slaughter her family and servants. As he most likely would have had she not had the courage to intervene.

Her belief in God, however, gave her the confidence to stand up in front of four hundred men and declare that letting God lead was a better path to follow. The result must have astonished those men. David listened to this humble woman, overwhelmed by her confidence and wisdom. His rage vanished; he called her blessed. After Nabal died, David further rewarded her by making Abigail his wife.

No matter what our gifts and talents, they are made even more powerful when put into action under God's guidance. Trusting Him, believing in His power within us, gives all believers the confidence to take action.

Get a Joy Infusion

"Do not sorrow, for the joy of the LORD is your strength."
NEHEMIAH 8:10 NKJV

*T*he Word tells us that the devil comes to steal and destroy (John 10:10)—and one of the things he loves to take from Christians is their joy. Do you know why? Because the joy of the Lord is our strength, and the devil knows that truth. He will do everything he can to take that strength from us.

That is why you have to be aware of the devil's crafty schemes for stealing your joy. For instance, if going to the congested grocery store on Saturday afternoon steals your joy, go shopping on a weekday evening or ask your spouse to make the Saturday run. If driving in rush-hour traffic stresses you out and steals your joy, try avoiding the crush by working out after quitting time and driving home later when the traffic has thinned. Or if you must drive at that crazy time of day, listen to praise and worship music while sitting in traffic.

You can do other things to help keep your joy at an optimum level, as well. Make sure you get enough sleep each night. Exercise on a regular basis. Eat a nutritionally balanced diet. Drink plenty of water. Don't overload your schedule with too many activities, which can lead to stress. Surround yourself with positive people. Finally, make time to laugh each day.

Ask God to give you a daily infusion of joy. Keep your heart and head full of the Word of God. Meditate on scriptures that deal with joy, such as:

- "You have put gladness in my heart, more than in the season that increased their grain and wine" (Psalm 4:7 NIV).

- "You make known to me the path of life; you will fill me with joy in your presence, with eternal pleasures at your right hand" (Psalm 16:11 NIV).

- "Restore to me the joy of your salvation and grant me a willing spirit, to sustain me" (Psalm 51:12 NIV).

God has an endless supply of joy awaiting you, and the devil can't steal it unless you let him. So keep hold of your joy–and refill your supply often.

Overcoming Fear with Love

. . . .

For God has not given us a spirit of fear,
but of power and of love and of a sound mind.
2 TIMOTHY 4:7 NKJV

$\mathcal{M}$rs. Eckles," the court clerk said, "we're ready for you."

These simple words changed Jan Eckles's life forever. Yet she had almost let fear keep her from hearing them. Most people are a bit nervous when starting a job, but Jan Eckles faced a few more obstacles than the average new employee. As an adult, a hereditary retinal disease had left her blind, and she had only recently learned to move about the city with a cane. She was also entering a brand-new field, that of court interpreter.

On that first day, an almost overwhelming sense of apprehension gripped Jan as she waited outside the courtroom. A sudden and sobering reality surged through her, making her feel inadequate with both her lack of experience as a Spanish interpreter and her limited knowledge of legal terminology. She was almost ready to back out when the court clerk came for her. Jan followed the clerk in, and with trembling hands and cramping stomach, she prepared for the frightening unknown.

That's when the promise Paul had written to Timothy rang in her ears: "For God has not given us a spirit of fear. . . ." The session began. She concentrated so intensely on each utterance that the pounding of the judge's gavel startled her. After ordering a recess, he asked Jan to approach the bench.

Painfully aware of her deficient abilities, Jan took a deep breath in preparation to receive a well-deserved reprimand. What she heard instead surprised her as much as the pounding gavel.

"Mrs. Eckles, I'm bilingual, as well," the judge said with a tender voice, "and I'm very impressed with the accuracy level of your interpretation and your professionalism."

With those words, Jan's new career took flight, and she heard in them not only the pleasure of the judge but the reassurance of God, as if He were reminding her, "If you trust in Me, the results exceed all your expectations."

Confidence from Encouraging Others

* * * * * * * * * * * * * * * * * * * *

*"You yourself have done this plenty of times,
spoken words that clarify, encouraged those who were about to quit.
Your words have put stumbling people on their feet,
put fresh hope in people about to collapse."*
JOB 4:3–4 MSG

I don't think I can do this." Elaine sat in the car, refusing to get out. I struggled with what to say, saying a little prayer for guidance. "What are you afraid of?" She shrugged. "I'm not sure it's fear. More like the embarrassment that makes you clean the house before the maid comes." She paused. "I feel like I should lose weight before joining a gym."

I almost laughed. Elaine had struggled with her weight for years, and here we were, about to go into a gym for the first time in more than twenty years. Elaine, however, now faced her fear of humiliation, in her words, "of being an old fat lady in front of all those young, hard bodies and skinny girls."

It seemed trivial to both of us, given the much larger issues in our lives. But Elaine's fear was real, and it threatened to be crippling, preventing her from making a much-needed change in her life. She needed encouragement; I wanted to offer to her the same help she'd so often given me in the past. It was then that this passage from Job came to mind, when Eliphaz reminded Job that he had so often encouraged his friends in the past, when their doubts had led them away from God. His words had helped them stay on the right path.

"Do you remember," I asked Elaine, "telling me over and over that I'm beautiful in the eyes of God, no matter what people here think?"

She cut her gaze toward me. She didn't want to hear this.

I grinned. "Your advice has always helped me when I had problems thinking straight, especially about God. You are one of the most confident women I know, about everything but this. You told me that confidence lies in God. Yes?"

Reluctantly, Elaine nodded.

"So why is it you think He'll support you with your hardest tasks but not give you the confidence to do something as simple as walking into a gym?"

We sat in the dark for a long time as Elaine stared out over the parking lot clustered with cars. "I guess," she said finally, "if He can help David and Job through their darkest times, He can help me face a few skinny girls."

We got out, thankful that God could give us the confidence to tackle any task, no matter how big–or small.

The Confidence to Save a Child

*When she could no longer hide him, she took an ark of bulrushes
for him, daubed it with asphalt and pitch, put the child in it,
and laid it in the reeds by the river's bank.*

EXODUS 2:3 NKJV

*I*magine carrying a precious child within you for nine months,
all the while knowing that if you gave birth to a boy, he would be
immediately killed on orders from the government.

Like every other Hebrew mother of her time, Jochebed knew that
her newborn son, Moses, would be murdered if she didn't take drastic
action. For the first three months after his birth, Jochebed hid her
squirmy child, but she knew she couldn't conceal him forever. So she
did exactly as the pharaoh commanded: "Every son who is born you
shall cast into the river" (Exodus 1:22 NKJV). Only this resourceful
mother went one step further, encasing her child in bulrushes and
pitch before slipping him into the water. On the bank, his sister kept a
close watch over her tiny brother.

Few believers today can understand the risks and fears of living
under the harsh conditions of the Hebrews under the pharaohs. Yet
Jochebed, as a daughter of Levi and married to a man of her own tribe,

must have known the promises of God. Choosing to follow her beliefs instead of the cruelty of her world, she stepped out in faith in an effort to protect her beautiful son. Her confidence in God allowed her to release Moses into the river, only to have him return to her arms as the protected grandson of the man who had wanted him dead. As a result, she delivered to the world one of its greatest leaders, and her entire family was blessed (see Numbers 26:59).

Although mothers today don't usually have to take such dire actions to protect our children, we are called upon to be advocates for them, to support and stand beside them, pray for them, and let them go when the time comes. All of which requires confidence in God's loving care and plan for our own lives—and that of each child born to us.

Harmony, Melody, and Rhythm

. . . .

Be filled with the Spirit; speaking to yourselves in psalms
and hymns and spiritual songs, singing and making melody
in your heart to the Lord.
EPHESIANS 5:18–19 KJV

*W*hile growing up and as a grown woman, I've always appreciated
my mother's humming. When she's working in the kitchen, cleaning,
or doing a project, she's humming. The only time it ceased for a
long season was in the first months or year after my dad died. But
as He does, God wrought His healing in my mom's brokenness, and
she's back to her humming self. One of the nurses I work with is a
hummer, too. I find it pleasant and even infectious.

One night at work I was mindlessly doing it, too, hardly
conscious of the sound I was making.

"Excuse me," said one of my coworkers. I looked up to face a
scowl. "Would you mind? That noise is very irritating."

So much for all of us enjoying someone else's humming. It must
be why God had Paul instruct believers to make a "melody *in your
heart* to the Lord" (emphasis added). Not everyone enjoys listening to
another's melodic musings.

Music in all its forms is a powerful motivator, isn't it? There's hardly a movie made that doesn't have music playing in the background. Hitler was quick to use music to rouse his armies to a passionate fervor for "the fatherland." We use lullabies to quiet infants and praise songs to inspire worship and focus on God. Even computer games and pinball machines have a "music" of sorts to engage the user.

Have you ever thought about how the Lord Jesus sounded when He sang? Before He and the disciples went out to the Mount of Olives, they sang a hymn (Mark 14:26). Did the Lord have a rich, low baritone or a soaring tenor voice? God has built music into creation because His was the first voice. Not only do the stars sing (Job 38:7), but God sings too. "The LORD your God is with you," Zephaniah says. "He. . .will rejoice over you with singing" (Zephaniah 3:17 NIV). The context of God singing over us in that verse is in an un-hurried moment of serenity. "He will quiet you with his love" (Zephaniah 3:17 NKJV).

In sign language, the gesture for singing or music is a fluid motion of one hand over another. That "says" music can be soothing. Is your day today hectic or out of control? It may be time to put on some music, put those fingers on the piano keys, or hum your favorite praise song. Let a little music breathe a measure of serenity into your hurried day.

God Is the Source of Your Strength

*My health may fail, and my spirit may grow weak,
but God remains the strength of my heart; he is mine forever.*
PSALM 73:26 NLT

$Susanna Wesley is the perfect example of how influential a mother
can be on not only her children but the world at large. Anyone
intimidated by the "good wife" of Proverbs 31 should take a second
look at Susanna, whose life can make most of us weak in the knees.

Born in 1669, Susanna was one of twenty-five children born to
Samuel Annesley, a minister who filled his house with a broad range
of people, some of them famous men of politics and academia. The
lively and crowded household was filled with debate and dissent, and
curious Susanna took it all in, learning Greek, Hebrew, theology, and
literature from her father and his friends.

In 1688 she married Samuel Wesley, a young Church of England
minister. The marriage was fruitful, if not particularly happy. The
first nineteen years of her marriage Susanna gave birth to nineteen
children, although nine of them died while still infants. Her home
burned twice, once almost taking five-year-old John with it. Her grief,
multiple births, and poor living conditions left the young woman

ill much of the time, but Susanna didn't give up or dwell on her hardships.

With money tight and her husband often gone, Susanna grew even more determined to give her children the kind of education and home life she had growing up. So began her Sunday evening meetings. In addition to the standard lessons she gave the children, these discussions centered around scripture reading and the sermons they had heard that morning. They were intended just for family, but word soon spread, and before long a crowd started showing up.

At a time when most women weren't allowed to speak in church, much less the pulpit, Susanna Wesley found the strength and confidence to speak to more than two hundred people every week. The profound impact her determination had on her children cannot be denied. Charles wrote more than eighteen hundred hymns, and her son John went on to change the face of Christianity. While Susanna's health was frequently weak, her strength and confidence came from the One who never fails.

Adoption

· ·

"For God so loved the world that he gave his one and only Son,
that whoever believes in him shall not
perish but have eternal life."
JOHN 3:16 NIV

Childbirth doesn't conjure up images of serenity for anyone. Especially for the mother-to-be.

Jennifer loves to tell the story of her son's birth. Unable to have children, Jennifer and her husband opted for a private adoption. Over the months of the pregnancy, they got to know the teenage birth mother well. When the actual date of delivery came, however, things did not go well. The mother had a prolonged labor, and the baby was face-up. Forceps had to be used, and the special care nursery team was called in to resuscitate the blue, depressed newborn. His late but lusty cry was music to the ears of his mother.

As one of the team members brought the howling, now pink infant back to the bedside, the obstetrician asked the exhausted patient he was stitching up one question.

"What's this big ten-pounder's name?"

With a voice weary from her task, but just as resolute, the young woman locked eyes with Jennifer.

"You'll have to ask his mother."

In that moment, holding Joshua in her arms for the first time, Jennifer wept tears of relief and joy. The years have not diminished the memory of the birth mother's loving act of selflessness that gave Jennifer her only son. Serenity replaced the hours of anxiety and fear.

How like God's unselfish love for us. God did not give His Son, Jesus Christ, to us or for us as we waited in eager expectation. Rather, He did for us what we could not do for ourselves. Just as Joshua's birth mother gave him to a woman powerless to birth her own son, God gave us His Son, Jesus Christ, when we were powerless to become members of His family. (See Romans 5:6; Galatians 4:4–5.)

Jennifer had to receive Joshua to be a mother. We must receive Jesus Christ to be Christians. The Bible tells us, "Just as you received Christ Jesus as Lord, continue to live in him, rooted and built up in him. . .overflowing with thankfulness" (Colossians 2:6–7). That's how we secure serenity with God. And, oddly enough, it's called. . . "adoption" (Ephesians 1:5 KJV).

There Is No "I" in TEAM

. . . .

You can easily enough see how this kind of thing works by looking
no further than your own body. Your body has many parts–limbs,
organs, cells–but no matter how many parts you can name,
you're still one body. It's exactly the same with Christ.

4 CORINTHIANS 12:12 MSG

*I*s your nickname "Tammy Takeover"? Do you try to do everything alone? If so, we should form a support group–because I also struggle with that I'll-just-do-it myself attitude.

Of course, that line of thinking isn't original. The world has been telling us for years, "If you want something done right, you have to do it yourself." So I decided I would. I tried to do it all–all by myself–all the time. I ended up overwrought, stressed, and mean. (Yes, just ask my husband. I so didn't have the joy of the Lord in my life.)

God didn't intend for us to go it alone. He even addresses that errant line of thinking in 4 Corinthians 12:12, using the human body as an example of teamwork. We are just one part of the big picture. We each play an important role, but we will never accomplish what God has for us if we try to do everything all alone. Why? Look to the verse for the answer: According to God's Word, we are just one part of the body. No matter what a great eyeball you are, you will never be able to hear, because you're not an ear!

So quit trying to be an ear! Be the best eyeball you can be, and work with the person in your life who was called to be an ear. Together, you will do much! Alone, you will just be a good eye– nothing more.

Teamwork, whether you are in an office setting or helping with vacation Bible school, is vitally important. Lose the "Tammy Takeover" mentality and do your part with the rest of the body, and big things can be accomplished in a short time. And the really great part is that you will be much happier! You will get to enjoy the experience and celebrate with the team members when "all of y'all" (Texan plural for "y'all") meet your goal! It's a win-win situation.

So go out and do your part, but don't try to do everyone else's part, too. If you feel yourself moving into the I-can-do-it-all-by-myself mode, ask God to keep you focused on what He has called you to do and nothing more. Remember, there is no "I" in TEAM–but there are great rewards and happiness when we choose to work as a team.

Is Your Glass Half Full?

*Rejoice always, pray without ceasing, in everything give thanks;
for this is the will of God in Christ Jesus for you.*
1 THESSALONIANS 5:16–18 NKJV

* * *

*A*re you a glass-half-empty or a glass-half-full person?

You might say that's a foolish question because, either way, it's just half a glass. Quantitatively, that's true. What you think doesn't increase or decrease the actual amount of liquid in the glass. But qualitatively it makes a huge difference–between an unhappy or a happy existence.

A few years ago, the media company I worked for experienced a difficult financial year. As the holidays approached, we received a memo that read, "Due to our challenging financial year, we are unable to give you, our treasured employees, Christmas bonuses this holiday season." The letter continued with a heartfelt apology, a plea for patience, and a prayer for a better new year.

When the infamous memo arrived on our desks, the glass-half-empty people were livid! To be honest, we glass-half-full folks weren't exactly doing the dance of Christmas joy, either–but the difference between the two groups' reactions was vast.

The glass-half-empty employees griped for months. If they were asked to do anything beyond the norm, they would grudgingly comply–then say something sarcastic like, "Yeah, we'd be happy to get right on that because our company has done so much for us lately." The glass-half-full folks, on the other hand, continued to work hard and hope for a better future.

The following December, we received another envelope on our desks, but this time it didn't contain just a memo. It held a memo and a Christmas bonus check. Sighs of relief and whoops of celebration rang out in the glass-half-full camp. Guess what the glass-half-empty group did?

They complained.

"Well, it's about time!" was heard from certain cubicles. Or, "Better late than never!" or "Too little too late, if you ask me."

It was a good lesson–one I'll never forget. I saw firsthand how glass-half-empty folks and glass-half-full people handle life's day-to-day ups and downs. The bottom line? I discovered that glass-half-full people live happier, fuller lives than the glass-half-empty folks. When faced with exactly the same circumstances, one group chose to be happy and the other depressed.

So I ask you again: Are you a glass-half-empty person or a glass-half-full person? If your glass looks half empty today, fill up on God and change your perspective. The level in your glass may not change, but your level of happiness will!

Courage to Change

· ·

*Don't copy the behavior and customs of this world,
but let God transform you into a new person by changing
the way you think. Then you will know God's will for you,
which is good and pleasing and perfect.*

Romans 12:2 NLT

As a motivational speaker, Tracy Hurst is a dynamic Bible teacher who uses humor and a down-to-earth personality to draw people to her message of the love and transforming power of Christ. As a Christian counselor and cohost of Moody Radio's "Marriage and Family Today" program, Tracy also works hard to help people call on the power of Christ to change their lives, to move away from the consequences of ill-made choices and into the life-altering light of God.

The success of Tracy's leadership comes, in part, because she has walked a few of those dark paths herself. She's been there. As a teenager, she was rebellious and angry. She fought a deep depression and even became suicidal. Then, at sixteen, she accepted Christ, which began a life transformation so dynamic that her story began to inspire others around her. She became a teen leader in her school and community. She fought her school board so she could lead a

Bible study at her high school, and she even led her own mother to the Lord. Her enthusiasm for the Lord continued as she went on to pursue both a bachelor's and master's degree in psychology. She worked for New Life Clinics, and today she has a counseling practice at the AlphaCare Christian Counseling Center.

Yet none of this would have been possible if Tracy had not allowed Christ to change her life through scripture. She writes, "Romans 12:2 made it clear that I was not going to know His will for my life until I allowed God to change the way I think. I needed to make the Word of God the final authority in my life. I am now in His perfect will as a Christian counselor, and I have the privilege of sharing this truth with my clients."

This verse gave Tracy Hurst the courage to change her life, and as a result she has been able to reach out to people all over the world, helping them change as well.

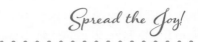

Spread the Joy!

∙ ∙

Love is kind.
1 CORINTHIANS 13:4 NIV

*E*very single day we encounter joy stealers. You know the type–rude cashiers, angry drivers, inconsiderate coworkers, and even grouchy family members. You'll have an opportunity (probably before breakfast) to get mad, but you can choose kindness instead. Not long ago I encountered one of those joy stealers at the supermarket.

This cashier was angry. I don't know why–maybe she'd had a fight with her husband before work, or maybe her boss had just given her crummy hours for the next week. Whatever the cause, this gal was not in a good mood. As she scanned my items, she was muttering under her breath. Though I hated to disturb her, I had a few coupons to use, which I slid toward her. Glaring at me, she snapped, "You're supposed to hand those to me at the beginning of the transaction." Ever been there?

Now, what I wanted to say was, "Listen, sister, I'll report your rudeness to your supervisor. Don't push me." But my heart wouldn't let me. Instead, I answered, "Oh, I'm sorry. I wasn't aware of that policy. If it's too much trouble, I can just save them and use them the next time I go grocery shopping." She didn't even respond, so I continued. "I bet you get tired of rule breakers like me, eh?"

She cracked a smile. "Some days it's an aggravating job," she shared in a much nicer tone.

"Well, I don't envy you," I added. "I used to work retail for a clothing store, and I know how the public can be. Some days I just wanted to scream."

"You've got that right," she chimed in.

Before she scanned my last can of green beans, we were best buddies. She not only let me use my coupons, but she gave me a couple of extra ones she had at her station. We chatted a bit more while she bagged my groceries, and then I told her to keep up the good work and try not to let the aggravation get to her. She smiled a full-out smile and said, "I'll try not to. . .and you come back and see me."

I didn't let this cashier steal my joy. Instead, I gave her some of mine. You can do the same. Joy is contagious. Be a carrier and spread it everywhere you go.

God Gives You Wisdom

*If any of you need wisdom, you should ask God, and it will be given
to you. God is generous and won't correct you for asking.*
JAMES 1:5 CEV

𝒯he older I've gotten, the more I've heard myself uttering the words,
"Well, as my mother used to say. . ." It's almost become a joke
among my friends, and they'll start to grin even before I can get some
pithy proverb out. In fact, some of my mother's sayings are quite
humorous, filled with homespun advice and earthy metaphors, like
the day she was canning some beans and told me she was "hotter than
a tent preacher in July." We're from Alabama, and I can assure you
that camp meetings in the summer can get pretty hot!

It's not just the down-to-earth proverbs, however, that I depend
on. My mother's wisdom sometimes amazes me. I began to ask her
advice on people and situations when I was still just a kid, and she has
seldom steered me wrong. When a kid was trying to bully me in junior
high school, her advice helped me ease the situation in just a few days.
When dealing with a variety of men in college had me spinning in
confusion, she helped me find my feet again. She taught me how to
handle money, work, even my faith.

I once asked her about the source of her wisdom, and she responded, "A little bit of living and a whole lot of prayer."

My mother had learned to rely on God for guidance and inspiration, which had made her invaluable to her friends and family. Even the tiniest problems were turned over to God, which gave her the confidence to help out those who came to her for advice.

I think it's very revealing that wisdom in scripture is portrayed as a woman (see Proverbs 4:20-24), since women seem to have an instinctual sense of how to take the little lessons of life and scripture and use them to nurture those they love. Even more encouraging is this reminder from James, that if we ever feel we're lacking in wisdom, all we have to do is ask–and God will provide both wisdom and the confidence to use it.

Let the Past Be the Past at Last

· · · · · · · · · · · · · · · · · · · ·

Forgetting what is behind and straining toward what is ahead,
I press on toward the goal to win the prize for which
God has called me heavenward in Christ Jesus.
PHILIPPIANS 3:13–14 NIV

*R*alph Waldo Emerson wrote: "Finish each day and be done with it. You have done what you could; some blunders and absurdities have crept in; forget them as soon as you can. Tomorrow is a new day; you will begin it serenely and with too high a spirit to be encumbered with your old nonsense." In other words, "Get over it! Move on! Tomorrow is another day!"

Okay, so you totally messed up yesterday. Maybe you yelled at your children, ate too many Twinkies, acted disrespectfully to your employer, or spoke sharply to your spouse. Whatever you did wrong yesterday, be quick to repent and move on. The devil will try to make you dwell on your past mistakes, but you don't have to go there. Once you have asked for forgiveness–both from those people you offended and from Jesus Christ–you're good to go! You get to start the next day with a clean slate.

God doesn't remember the mistakes you have confessed, so

why should you? Don't let yesterday's blunders steal today's joy. Remember, guilt and condemnation are not from the Father. So if you are experiencing those emotions, realize their origin–they come from the devil. He wants you to feel so bad about yourself that you will never move forward. Know why? Because the devil understands the awesome plans God has for your life, and he doesn't want you to enjoy your bright future. The enemy will do anything he can to keep you in your past, so don't fall for his tricks. Instead, learn from your mistakes and move on.

Let the past be the past at last! Praise the Lord for His unending mercy and love, and ask Him to help you become more like Him. You are a work in progress. We are all like spiritual babies, learning to walk and occasionally falling down–and that's okay. Quit glancing back at your blunders; keep your eyes on Jesus. Your future is happy and bright in Him.

Get Over It!

*Then Rachel said, "I have had a great struggle
with my sister, and I have won."*
GENESIS 30:8 NIV

*O*ur ladies' Bible study group, studying Genesis, had come to the scripture portion about Jacob and his dysfunctional family. The writer of the study asked us to consider how we might individually counsel sisters Rachel and Leah, Jacob's competing wives. As women living in another culture and thousands of years removed from these two sisters, we each grappled with an answer—except for one gal in our group. We all wanted to hear what Cheryl, a Christian counselor with years of experience, had to say.

Cheryl listened without comment to our speculative answers. Thankfully, none of us has ever had to share our husband's affection or admiration with "sister wives." Our answers probably wouldn't have made a dent in the dynamics of this fractured family, but the question really made us think. What about Cheryl? What would be a professional Christian counselor's response to each sister? "I'd ask them both the same question," she said. That set all of us back. None of us had thought to pose a question first. "This is it. 'How is this competition helping you achieve your goal?' "

Whoa. Unloved wife Leah, doing what increased her stature and Jacob's in their culture (having lots of boy babies), wanted her husband's love. Childless Rachel, loved adoringly by Jacob, wanted to have his children. Each woman took out her frustration on her sister. Neither found contentment in what she had. She only found frustration in what she lacked. But how was their competition helping Rachel conceive? How was it aiding Leah in her desire to win her husband's heart?

Are you giving yourself to a competition that won't help you achieve your goal? Do you allow situations over which you have no control to drag you into a cycle of frustration, anger, or self-pity? The Bible never tells us if Rachel and Leah were able to get beyond their competition to a place of contentment. But the question remains for us to answer if some rivalry holds our serenity at bay. A sincere prayer to the God who can give us real contentment may get us started. Try paraphrasing 2 Thessalonians 3:16. "Lord of peace, please give me your peace no matter what happens."

To Follow God's Call

. . . .

And Deborah, a prophetess, the wife of Lapidoth,
she judged Israel at that time.
JUDGES 4:4 KJV

*T*hroughout scripture, the faith women have in God provides them with the confidence to stand up for their beliefs, face down armies, and deal with the pressures of their lives. One woman is even called to guide ten thousand men into battle.

The only woman to sit as a judge over Israel, Deborah's most vital relationships are introduced in this first mention of her. The prophets in Old Testament times were men and women called by God to communicate His will to the people. Thus, Deborah already had a strong relationship with the Lord when she was called to sit as judge for Israel at a time of harsh oppression. She was also a wife, with an established household and place in her world. Yet in a society that did not always value women as leaders, she answered God's call on her life.

Using her wisdom to settle disputes for her people, however, is a far cry from leading them into battle against an army featuring nine hundred iron chariots, vehicles that had revolutionized warfare and forced the Israelites to seek refuge in fortified cities. Jabin, the king in Canaan, had dealt harshly with the Israelites for more than twenty years, using his army to keep them under his rule. Finally, they cried out to God for relief in what appeared to be an impossible situation to overcome.

Deborah, however, had the ability to see beyond the current situation. She was a woman of vision, and she called on Barak to do as the Lord had commanded, to take his troops and prepare to face Sisera, Jabin's general, in a battle to save their people. Barak's response—that he would do so only if she was with him (see Judges 4:8)—underscores the trust Israel had placed in the woman God had called for them.

God always looks for women who are ready to embrace His vision for their lives, their family, and even their nation. Such women of vision have the courage that enables them to conquer and overcome in situations that would otherwise seem unconquerable.

Words of Wisdom from Eleanor Roosevelt

· ·

As God's chosen people, holy and dearly loved,
clothe yourselves with compassion, kindness,
humility, gentleness and patience.
COLOSSIANS 3:12 NIV

Eleanor Roosevelt has been called the most revered woman of her generation. She made a difference every place she ever dwelled. She not only gave birth to six children, but she also served as a dynamic political helpmate to her husband, Franklin Delano Roosevelt.

Eleanor Roosevelt literally transformed the role of First Lady, holding press conferences, traveling to all parts of the country, giving lectures and radio broadcasts, and expressing her opinions in a daily syndicated newspaper column called "My Day." You might say that she was a spitfire, a woman on a mission, a servant to humankind, a loving wife and mother, and a role model for all women.

Knowing of her accomplishments, it was very interesting to discover Mrs. Roosevelt was a very shy and awkward child. Her mother died when she was only eight years old, and her father died just two years later. It wasn't until she began attending a distinguished school in England that she began to develop self-confidence. During that self-discovery phase, she wrote, "No matter how plain a woman may be, if truth and loyalty are stamped upon her face, all will be attracted to her."

What wise words from such a young teen, huh? If only we all understood that truth. For years, society has told us that if we're not beautiful—like the cover girls on magazines—then we have no place in this world. Many women feel they don't have a voice because they don't fit into a size 6 suit. Many of us have bought the lie. But no more!

Like Eleanor Roosevelt, we, too, can overcome our shyness and change our world. Have you ever met someone who isn't really that physically attractive, but after you're around that person for any length of time, you see her as lovely? That's the same quality Eleanor Roosevelt understood. She got it! It's not what's on the outside that makes us worthy, lovely, and attractive. That kind of beauty is fleeting. It's that loyalty, truth, and love on the inside of us, spilling out onto others, that draws people to us. In other words, it's the Jesus in us that makes us irresistible.

If you're feeling plain, unworthy, unattractive, and unnoticed— give yourself a makeover from the inside out. Ask God to develop the fruit of the Spirit within you, and allow the Lord to fill you with His love. Soon you'll be confident and irresistible—just like Eleanor Roosevelt. And you'll make a difference every place you go!

The Confidence to Be Used by God

· ·

And Mary said: "My soul glorifies the Lord and my spirit rejoices in God my Savior, for he has been mindful of the humble state of his servant. From now on all generations will call me blessed."
LUKE 1:46–48 NIV

What if Mary had said no? She could have. God didn't make her accept His will for her life; He let her choose. As overwhelming as the appearance of an angel in her room must have been, Mary's choice should not have been an easy one. Her life was simple and stable: She was young, engaged to a good man, and ready to start her own home. Accepting God's will for her meant risking all of that, and much more.

A woman who became pregnant during her betrothal could be accused of adultery and stoned. At the very least, Joseph would know that the child was not his and break off his commitment to her. If she survived, her life would be ruined. Mary's mind, however, was on the Lord, not human society. She stood in awe of such an honor and asked only how God planned to achieve this miracle. When she sang her praises of the Lord later (see Luke 1:46–55), this young girl expressed her joy and pride in being chosen by God. Her love of God and understanding of scriptures gave her complete confidence in her unhesitant "Yes, Lord!"

Mary was indeed blessed, but being Jesus' mother also came with tremendous anxiety and heartache. She saw the glory of His miracles but also felt the pain of His death. Like any mother, she panicked when He went missing and rejoiced in His triumphs. And after His death, she joined His disciples in the upper room (see Acts 1:12–14) to pray, grieve, and be with those who loved Him.

Mary could have said no, the same as any of us who feel God's tug on our lives. As Mary discovered, following God can lead us down a path filled with great pain as well as tremendous joy. Yet if we love Him and understand His love for us, then we will discover the confidence to say yes!

God Hears You

. . . .

And this is the confidence that we have in him, that,
if we ask any thing according to his will, he heareth us:
and if we know that he hear us, whatsoever we ask,
we know that we have the petitions that we desired of him.

1 JOHN 5:14–15 KJV

"Maybe you're praying for the wrong thing." Marilee's gentle voice and soft tone let me know she didn't intend to be critical.

"What do you mean?" I asked. Since returning to our church following my divorce, Marilee had been a mentor and a good friend.

"Maybe it's not in His will for her to be healed."

Ah. Not an easy thing for a mother to hear. My daughter, her disabilities caused at birth by a lack of oxygen, grinned up at us from her bed. Marilee, her godmother and frequent caregiver, loved her almost as much as I did. For me, a desire for Rachel's healing grew directly from that love. Wouldn't God want the same thing?

"Maybe," answered Marilee, "but maybe not. After all, He looks at the heart, the mind, and the spirit. Not the body." She reminded me of this passage in 1 John. "Maybe He has a plan for her that doesn't involve walking around and going to school. Healing is your will for her, but it might not be His."

How frustrating! I chafed, rebelled, and argued with God for weeks about this. Then, one Sunday I observed Rachel through a glass panel in the nursery door. The church had placed a cot in the toddler's nursery so Rachel could lie down and watch her videos during church. The toddlers sat next to her, petting her, offering her toys. When I went in, they asked dozens of questions: "Why can't she walk? Why won't she answer me? What's wrong with her? Is she sick? Will she get better?"

That night, I went to my knees with a new prayer, asking this time for help in following His will: "Lord, she is Your child. Use her as You see fit. Just give me a clue on how to help You care for her."

That prayer has been answered in more ways than I can possibly count. Rachel's presence in our church brought greater awareness of persons with disabilities to the entire congregation. I've written and published a number of articles about Rachel's life and God's blessings on us both. I've spoken about her to church groups. While Rachel's health has been a furious roller coaster ride, she has persevered. The doctors told me she might live until she was eight or nine.

She's now eighteen—and I'm still praying, with the full confidence that God is listening carefully.

The Confidence to Follow Christ Unceasingly

. . . .

Early on Sunday morning, while it was still dark,
Mary Magdalene came to the tomb and found that
the stone had been rolled away from the entrance.
JOHN 20:1 NLT

*M*ary couldn't wait. Her unwavering loyalty to Christ continued, even though He had died on the cross. She arose well before dawn and went to His grave to anoint His body with burial spices (see Mark 16:1), as one last task she could do for her Lord. Her discovery of the open tomb led to astonishment and grief, as she assumed the Romans had taken Him away. She ran to tell Peter and the "other disciple, whom Jesus loved," and they, too, saw that His body was gone, but they simply returned to their homes. Mary waited.

Throughout the New Testament, while most of those around Jesus doubted, denied, or fled, Mary and some of the other women stayed by His side. They traveled with the disciples during good times, and they helped support Jesus' ministry financially (see Luke 8:1–3). Mary's devotion began the moment He freed her from seven demons, and she didn't abandon Him or her faith when His journey turned toward the crucifixion. She was not afraid of being associated with Jesus, and she followed him up Golgotha and down again to the tomb. The reward for this devotion came as she waited by the empty tomb, weeping.

Spotting a man she thought was the gardener, she begged for information about Jesus. Instead, she heard the voice she thought was gone forever. "'Sir,' she said, 'if you have taken him away, tell me where you have put him, and I will go and get him.' 'Mary!' Jesus said. She turned to him and cried out, 'Rabboni!'" (John 20:15–16 NLT).

Mary Magdalene was the first person to see Jesus after His resurrection, the first to know that the prophecies were true, the first to discover that Christ was alive forever. Rejoicing, she ran to tell others of the good news. Mary's loyalty reminds us that devoting our lives to the Lord isn't always simple. Allegiance to God takes determination as well as love.

Many times, believers will lose the intensity they felt after their conversion, or they'll devote prayer time to God only when they need something. Giving ourselves to Him, however, is the least we can do for the One who gave Himself so totally to us.

To Instruct the Ones We Love

. . . .

She kissed them, and they lifted up their voices and wept.
And they said to her, "Surely we will return
with you to your people."
RUTH 1:9–10 NKJV

*A*lthough believing women are encouraged to mentor other women (see Titus 2:3–5), there are few examples of women actually doing that in scripture.

Naomi, however, mentored her daughter-in-law Ruth with love and respect as well as a touch of necessity. A woman of great courage, Naomi left all that she knew twice in her life. First, when a famine struck Judah, she moved with her husband, Elimelech, and their two sons to Moab. They did well there, and after Elimelech died, her sons married Moabite women, Orpah and Ruth. The family thrived for the next ten years, until both sons died as well, leaving the three women widowed and desperate.

Weighing her choices, Naomi decided her best option lay with returning to her family in Judah. The famine had passed, and she had relatives who could help her. She encouraged Orpah and Ruth to return to their fathers' houses, where they could find warmth and support, as well. Neither of the younger women wanted to go. What a testimony to the bonding love these women must have felt for each other!

Finally, Orpah relented and left, but Ruth stayed, pleading with her mother-in-law with some of the most beautiful words of commitment in history (see Ruth 1:16–17). Not only was Ruth willing to give up her friends, family, and home, but she was also giving up her gods. She chose the Lord, turning her life to Him because of the work she'd seen Him do in the lives of Naomi and her family. Naomi led Ruth to God by just loving Him, worshipping Him, and relying on Him.

Naomi's mentoring of Ruth continued once they returned to Judah. Ruth, a stranger, knew nothing of the ways of her new land. Naomi guided her, told her exactly what to do, where to go, and what to say. Ruth trusted her and obediently did as her mother-in-law instructed. As a result, Naomi's kinsman Boaz took Ruth as his wife, and their son became an ancestor of Jesus Christ.

Mature believers know that one of the best ways to reach other people for the Lord is to let them see His work in their lives and how much they love Him. Although Naomi grieved over some of the events in her life, especially the loss of her husband and sons (see Ruth 1:20), she never gave up hope nor stopped loving and worshipping God.

God Is Your Confidence

*Do not be afraid of sudden terror, nor of trouble from
the wicked when it comes; for the LORD will be your confidence,
and will keep your foot from being caught.*
PROVERBS 3:25–26 NKJV

The first thing Linda Evans Shepherd noticed as the shock of the accident wore off was the silence.

Her ears still rang from the shattering impact of the other vehicle hitting hers, and adrenaline still pumped through her veins. She was trembling but unhurt as she scrambled to pull herself away from the mangled car, one thought occupying her mind. Why wasn't her daughter crying?

Eighteen-month-old Laura had been strapped securely in her car seat behind Linda, but the crash had severed her car, and Linda felt terror and panic surge through her as she twisted around. Laura was gone.

At that moment, Linda, a well-known Christian writer and speaker, faced the horror of a mother's worst nightmare. She scrambled through the wreckage, finally finding Laura, still in her seat, face-down on the pavement. The brain damage she sustained would leave her in a coma for eleven months. And, as Linda sat vigil by her daughter's bed, twenty-seven "experts" came and went, telling Linda that Laura would remain in a vegetative state for the rest of her life.

Linda, however, never gave up hope on Laura–or God–no matter how much fear she felt for her child. She felt Him leading her as her daughter's advocate, and Linda's confidence in God's support and answered prayers gave her the strength to continue to push for care– and to believe.

While Laura's brain damage was permanent, her vegetative state was not. Today she is a glorious teenager who plays, communicates, and loves with a purity that makes her a living example of God's unconditional affection for all His children. As Linda writes, "Laura, like other disabled people, has a purpose. For it's not about ability, it's about love. Laura fulfills her purpose better than anyone I know." And Linda's faith-based confidence shines as proof of God's guidance through even the most mind-numbing fears.

God Builds You Up

*Perhaps you think we're saying these things just
to defend ourselves. No, we tell you this as Christ's servants,
and with God as our witness. Everything we do,
dear friends, is to strengthen you.*

2 CORINTHIANS 12:19 NLT

"You can do this. Take a deep breath—no, not that deep!"

The young woman in front of me was so nervous that her convention name tag quivered. "I don't think I'll get through it without throwing up on her shoes!"

We were both waiting for an appointment with an editor at a major publishing house. In less than ten minutes, we had to explain what our books were about and convince the editor that they would sell to readers. Writers make these kinds of pitches frequently, but each time, we almost feel as if our careers are on the line. The next ten minutes will make or break us.

I grabbed my friend's hand. "Listen to me. We practiced this. You know this story better than anyone and you love it. Tell it like you love it. Trust yourself. Trust your heart. Trust God."

She stared at me a moment, then nodded. "Pray with me."

In a lot of jobs, there is more competition than support. I've not found this to be true among writers, however, especially romance writers. They gather, support each other's efforts, hold workshops, share information about agents and publishers, and, best of all, praise each other. They build each other up.

This is what Paul was trying to do for the Corinthians in his second letter to them. Paul didn't write in order to bring attention to himself; instead, he used the authority God gave him to teach the Corinthians, to attempt to move them closer to Christ so they could grow in the faith.

God wants this for all of His children. He gave us His Word for our edification, as well as great teachers to help us grow and understand our faith and how it works in our everyday lives. He wants us to succeed, and He will send the right mentors and teachers to help us, just as he sent Paul to the Corinthians. With His support, we should have the confidence to step out toward whatever challenge awaits us.

Confidence after Loss

. . . .

"And if I go and prepare a place for you, I will come back
and take you to be with me
that you also may be where I am."
JOHN 14:3 NIV

One of the most difficult challenges we face in this life is dealing
with the loss of someone we love. It was this agony that plummeted
writer and teacher Jennifer Stephens to an all-time spiritual low
during the Christmas season of 2000.

Jennifer and her father had always had a special bond. When he
died on December 23 after a brief illness, the shock of his sudden
passing was magnified because she was four months pregnant with her
first child–a child who would never know the special man who would
have been her grandfather.

For Jennifer, the loss left a huge, gaping hole in her life. She
had never imagined life without her father. Now he was gone, and
she grieved that her unborn child would never have the chance to
have a special relationship with him. Jennifer had seen her father
interact many times with her nephew, and she knew what a wonderful
grandpa he was. She had desperately wanted that for her baby as

well. Life went on, however, and Jennifer muddled through the next few months feeling lonelier and lonelier even though her husband remained close, reaching out to her.

Then on June 28, 2004, after twenty-two hours of labor, Jennifer gave birth to her daughter. Yet the joy she and her husband felt was tempered when, only an hour later, they discovered that their beautiful child had a cleft palate. While not a life-threatening illness, it was still an unexpected challenge for the new parents, and more than ever, Jennifer missed her dad.

As the new parent of a child with a special need, she needed his counsel, his parenting wisdom. Looking for that comfort, she turned to her Bible, opening it to a bookmarked passage that had been read at her dad's funeral: "And if I go and prepare a place for you. . ."

With a sudden sense of peace, Jennifer realized that her dad had just gone on ahead of her, getting things ready for when she will go home to her Father's house. One day she will be with her father again. One day Jesus and her dad will come for her and they will take her home to the place prepared just for her. This knowledge gave Jennifer the courage and the confidence to go forward, sharing with her daughter the memories and the faith of a special man.

Claiming God's Promise

. . . .

And the LORD spake unto Moses, saying, The daughters of Zelophehad speak right: thou shalt surely give them a possession of an inheritance among their father's brethren; and thou shalt cause the inheritance of their father to pass unto them.
NUMBERS 27:6–7 KJV

$\mathcal{W}$hat astonishing confidence the five daughters of Zelophehad had in God's provisions for women!

Imagine the courage required for Mahlah, Noah, Hoglah, Milcah, and Tirzah to stand up before their entire community and ask their leaders to deviate from the established legal tradition as they petitioned: "Why should the name of our father be removed from among his family because he had no son? Give us a possession among our father's brothers" (Numbers 27:4 NKJV).

The laws God gave to the Hebrews following the Exodus were essential in not only maintaining law and order in the community but the property rights for each individual. This was crucial in ensuring that a family endured and prospered. Normally, such property passed through the sons. But what happened if there were no sons?

Zelophehad was a descendant of Joseph, making his lineage

vital to the community. While he died without sons, he did leave behind five daughters. According to the existing law, Zelophehad's possessions were to pass to his brothers. Instead, these five women stepped out in faith and appealed to Moses so that their father's name and lineage could continue.

When Moses then turned to God for an answer, the Lord agreed with the daughters of Zelophehad, then went a step further: "If a man dies and has no son, then you shall cause his inheritance to pass to his daughter" (Numbers 27:8 NKJV). Only if a man had no children at all would his brothers inherit. In a patriarchal society in which women had few rights, this was a radical change. Far from being a minor legal matter that was resolved in a few moments, this God dictated shift in Hebrew law reveals exactly how much He cares for women.

Here Comes the Judge

. . . .

I can do all this through him who gives me strength.
PHILIPPIANS 4:13 NIV

$\mathscr{D}$o you ever worry about what others think of you? I've found that most women struggle with this issue of being judged–even gorgeous, "got it all together" women. One of my dearest friends is absolutely beautiful. Would you believe that even she worries what others think of her? I once heard her say, "I'd love to do more teaching, but I'm just not ready."

I started thinking, *Wow, if she's not ready, nobody is ready.* I've never met anyone who studies the Word of God more than she does. So I said, "You are so ready. You probably have more of God's Word on the inside of you than anyone else I know." With that, she lowered her head and sighed. I had touched on something that upset her.

"What's the problem?" I pushed.

"Well, I have to lose at least fifteen more pounds before I'll be ready. I worry that everyone will be looking at how big my behind is rather than focusing on the message God's given me to speak."

I couldn't believe my ears. The devil had so deceived her. She had become so worried about what others would think of her that she wasn't walking in the fullness of God. She wasn't allowing herself to be used by Him.

As I drove home that day, I began to think back on all of the times I'd allowed my worries to keep me from serving God. I thought about specific instances when I'd been so afraid of being judged by others that I had completely missed an opportunity to serve Him. It made me sad–not just for me, but for all of my sisters in Christ who had done the same thing.

Are you one of those sisters? Have you been allowing your insecurities and fear of being judged to keep you from doing great things for God? If so, don't be sad. Just give those concerns to God and ask Him to fill you up with His love and confidence. Remind yourself throughout the day that you can do all things through Christ who gives you strength, and then go forward and change the world. You have much to offer!

Confidence to Speak the Word

* *

*"Now, Lord, look on their threats, and grant to Your servants
that with all boldness they may speak Your word, by stretching
out Your hand to heal, and that signs and wonders may be done
through the name of Your holy Servant Jesus." And when they
had prayed, the place where they were assembled together was
shaken; and they were all filled with the Holy Spirit,
and they spoke the word of God with boldness.*
ACTS 4:29–31 NKJV

Evangelism is not one of my gifts. I've known that for a long time.
God has blessed me many times over in my life: I'm a writer, a
teacher, sometimes a speaker. I have a child who is the light of my
life and friends whose support never wavers. The joy that being a
woman of Christ has brought me seems endless. Yet speaking about
those blessings has never been easy for me, and I've often prayed for
confidence with this, especially where those friends are concerned.

Because of my background and various interests, many of
my friends are not Christian. Some of them live rather wild,
undisciplined–and often lost–lives. They know I'm a Christian, and
they respect that. Yet I'm well aware that they don't want to hear

about God and His Son.

When I found this passage, I turned instead to prayer: "Give me the strength to speak of You, Lord–and even more, the right doors." The answer I received over and over to this prayer has been: *live it*. Instead of preaching or witnessing, I am to be the best Christian I know how. When I do, my friends begin to feel more comfortable asking me questions about my faith. When God moved the heart of a woman I'd known for more than ten years, she called me with questions about scripture and the ways God moves in our lives. Today she's an active member of a local church and a firm believer that she is where God wants her to be.

Not long after she joined the church, my phone rang late one night, just as I was preparing for bed. A mutual friend, witnessing the changes he'd seen in our friend, had some questions about Jesus Christ. We talked until after two in the morning.

Perhaps I'm never meant to reach thousands with my words or speak to hundreds about my faith. But through this prayer in Acts, I've found the confidence to reach out with my faith, one friend at a time.

Courage to Face the Darkness

* *

Your word is a lamp to my feet and a light to my path.
PSALM 119:105 NKJV

When Jan Eckles was thirteen, she was diagnosed with symptoms of retinitis pigmentosa (RP). This hereditary disease affects the retina of the eye, causing it to deteriorate slowly. The ophthalmologist she saw at the time, however, told her she would probably see no significant changes until she was sixty or older.

Jan was stunned at age twenty-seven, then, when a doctor told her she should no longer drive a car. Pregnant with her second child, her first reactions were anger and denial. Jan continued to drive for another five years, until she lost so much of her peripheral vision that she finally realized she was putting herself and her children in danger. Ultimately, her vision closed in completely, leaving her devastated. She writes of the experience:

"When a black curtain fell on my world, its darkness swallowed my dreams of a life of fulfillment and joy. I refused to face this reality, but the hereditary retinal disease forced me through the seasons of painful adjustments. The spring of hope as I desperately looked for treatments, transplants, medications, or vitamins. But the summer's hot rays of disappointments scorched all hope for a cure. The fall brought unavoidable changes–in my plans, my dreams, and activities.

"And finally the winter with its cold and cruel sentence to a dark prison labeled 'blind for life.' My emotional world darkened as well with the desperate longing to have my life normal as before. My blindness robbed my sons of a mom who could care for them. I anguished knowing my husband no longer had a wife who could do her part for the family. I prayed feverishly, 'Lord, what will I do? How can I make my life worthwhile. . .help me to go on. . .to survive in a sighted world.' "

Jan was ready to give up, but God was not ready to give up on her. When she was at her lowest, that's when God came into her heart, reminding her that spiritual illumination has an eternal, never-failing source to light her path. That "light" gave her the strength and courage to face her blindness, adapt, and move on to a much brighter future.

Her physical surroundings remain in the dark, but her life now shines under the light of God's Word. Our lives can, too–when we put our trust in God.

You Will Walk the Highest Hills

*The Sovereign LORD is my strength; he makes my feet like
the feet of a deer, he enables me to go on the heights.*

HABAKKUK 3:19 NIV

𝒯he sun rose, although I barely noticed. I had slept little, and my
body felt numb.

I knew that physically I was all right. Yet my world had closed in
with a darkness that had left me remote from any feelings. Emotions
of any kind–anger, love, even self-pity–seemed like foreign concepts
to my mind, which was devoid of most thought. Even the slightest
movement appeared to be impossible.

In the distance, I could hear my daughter stirring in her bed.
She would soon need breakfast and a diaper change. Responsibility
beckoned. *I have to get up*, I told myself, and almost as a last straw,
I prayed for help.

For no apparent reason, my mind then flashed to the phrase
"hind's feet in high places." I knew it well. Habakkuk's hymn of faith
is one of the most beautiful passages in the Bible. He was looking
back on the destruction of the land and the people of Israel caused
by the Babylonian invasion. This bleak time was one of hopelessness

and depression, a time when many could have easily walked away from their faith and their God. The prophet, however, put things in perspective, reminding us all that no matter how bad things get, God is always in control, always ready to help and aid us.

As someone who deals with stark cycles of depression, I had relied on these verses before. On days when simply getting out of bed to care for my disabled daughter requires a proactive and determined effort, I find trusting that God will lift me again to be one of the more encouraging aspects of my life.

Because He has lifted me, and I have stood on those high places. I cherish those memories, and I hold them as reminders that no matter how bad the darkness is today, next month or next year will be different, better, lighter. For me, these lovely verses are not simply words of love and understanding. They are also cherished words of hope.

A Selfless Vessel

· ·

Love is patient and kind. Love is not
jealous or boastful or proud.
1 CORINTHIANS 13:4 NLT

$\mathcal{M}$y neighbor Melanie is definitely a dog lover. She and her
husband have two "little boys"–Rupert and Jackson. They are the
most adorable little fluff balls you've ever seen. And let me tell you,
these puppies are treated like royalty. I often meet the couple taking
"the boys" on their evening jaunt, and we'll chat about our precious
puppies. (I have three adorable miniature long-haired dachshunds.)

Not long ago, Melanie told me that she had decided to adopt
a little girl dog to join in the fun. She had seen a Humane Society
advertisement in the local paper, and this little poodle mix named
Peaches had captured Mel's heart. She went on to say, "I couldn't bear
the thought of this little poodle being put down." So Mel adopted
Peaches and took her to the veterinarian for all of her necessary shots.

As it turned out, Peaches had a bad case of kennel cough, so Mel
had to leave her at the vet's for a week or so. But every single day, Mel
would go to the vet's office and play with Peaches, petting her and
talking nice to her. She wanted Peaches to know she would be loved at

her new home. The two bonded.

On the day that Mel was supposed to bring Peaches home, she overheard the veterinarian talking to a woman who was looking for a dog to be a companion for her elderly father. He lived in a retirement home, and his beloved cocker spaniel had recently passed away, leaving him very lonely and depressed.

As Mel listened to the woman's story, she knew what she had to do. Peaches was needed somewhere else–even though Mel already loved that little poodle as if she'd owned her for years. As the delighted and grateful woman left the veterinarian's office with Peaches under her arm, Mel sobbed. But she wasn't crying because she was sad. She was crying tears of joy because she knew God had truly used her that day.

She had been the selfless vessel He needed to make an old man's dream come true. A selfless heart is a rare and beautiful thing today, but you can always spot the ones who have such hearts. They seem to glow with goodness. So have you done any selfless acts lately? Are you available to be that selfless vessel for God? In this dog-eat-dog world, God needs us to glow with goodness. Be a selfless vessel today.

Also From Barbour Publishing

WHEN JESUS SPEAKS TO A WOMAN'S HEART

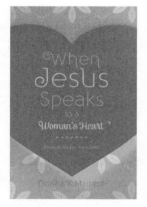

ISBN 978-1-63058-360-6

Available Wherever Christian
Books Are Sold!